So schön ist unser Land
Tag für Tag

Beautiful Germany – Day by Day

So schön ist unser Land
Tag für Tag

Beautiful Germany – Day by Day

Gerhard Launer

KNESEBECK

Vorwort

Seit über zwanzig Jahren eröffnet Gerhard Launer dem staunenden Betrachter mit seinen inzwischen über 100.000 Aufnahmen aus der Luft einen neuen Blick auf die Schönheiten unseres Landes.
Eine solche Leistung kann nur ein Mann mit außergewöhnlichen Fähigkeiten erbringen.
Gerhard Launer wollte eigentlich Geiger werden. Mit 14 Jahren studierte er neben der Schule am Konservatorium in Würzburg. Ein Autounfall beendete diesen Traum abrupt. Doch ließ er sich in der Ausbildung seiner Kreativität nicht beirren und studierte Grafikdesign, lernte Fotografieren, machte die Lizenz als Berufspilot und wurde Luftbildfotograf. So vereinte er das musische Talent und den Sinn für schöne Bilder mit einem großen technischen Können.
Heute sitzt er ganz allein bis zu acht Stunden in seinem Flugzeug, einer Cessna, auf der Suche nach dem besonderen Bild. Wenn ein passendes Motiv in Sicht ist, folgt virtuose Feinarbeit, bei der es auf Sekunden ankommt: Mit seinem Steuerknüppel in der linken und dem Fernauslöser in der rechten Hand, muss er den perfekten Moment festhalten.
Gerhard Launers Leidenschaft gilt dabei den Besonderheiten und Strukturen der Natur.
Er entdeckt ungewöhnliche Formationen und faszinierende Lichtstimmungen. Er liebt vor allem die frühen Abendstunden, in denen die Landschaft in fast unwirkliche Farben getaucht ist. Gerhard Launer entführt uns so in fantastische Welten und traumhafte Kompositionen. Ebenso entdecken wir auf seinen Bildern die großen uns allen bekannten Städte, berühmte Schlösser und Burgen ebenso wie Inseln oder typische Landstriche. Kurze Texte begleiten die Bilder und unterhalten uns mit wissenswerten Informationen über Deutschland. Lernen Sie mit Gerhard Launer unser Land neu kennen, und lassen Sie sich von einem Meister der Fotografie Tag für Tag mit einer neuen Bildkomposition überraschen.

Foreword

For more than twenty years Gerhard Launer has been captivating observers with his collection of now over 100,000 aerial photographs and opening their eyes anew to the beauty of our country.
This achievement is the mark of a man with exceptional talent. Gerhard Launer originally wanted to be a violinist and, at the age of 14, attended the Würzburg Conservatory alongside school. This dream was abruptly shattered by a car accident. He was undeterred in his creative development, however, and studied graphic design, took up photography, gained his professional pilot's licence and became an aerial photographer. By doing so, he combined his artistic talent and an appreciation of beautiful images with great technical aptitude. Today he sits alone for up to eight hours a day in his Cessna plane looking for that perfect shot. When a suitable motif is in view, he demonstrates virtuosic sleight of hand and a spot-on sense of timing. With the control stick in his left hand and the remote control release for his camera in his right hand, he strives to capture that perfect moment. In doing so, Gerhard Launer is passionate about the peculiarities and structures of nature. He discovers unusual formations and fascinating light effects. His favourite time of day is early evening when the countryside is bathed in almost unreal colours. Gerhard Launer transports us into fanciful worlds and fantastical compositions. By doing so, we rediscover through his pictures big cities – familiar to all of us –, famous palaces and castles as well as islands or typical stretches of land. Short texts accompany the pictures and provide us with useful information about Germany. Get to know our country afresh with Gerhard Launer and allow this master of photography to surprise you with a new image every day.

1

Januar

Alpenvorland, Bayern:
Die Passagiere im Heißluftballon blicken auf die 120 Kilometer entfernte Kette der Bayerischen Alpen. Der Ballon befindet sich etwa auf Höhe von Burgheim bei Neuburg an der Donau.

Alpenvorland, Bavaria. The passengers in the hot-air balloon look out on the mountains of the Bavarian Alps, 120 km away. The balloon is roughly on the level of Burgheim, close to Neuburg on the Danube.

2

January

München, Bayern: Im 10. und 11. Jh. ließen sich Mönche aus dem Kloster Tegernsee am Isarufer nieder. Aus der Mönchssiedlung »Munichen« entstand die heutige, 1,2 Millionen Einwohner zählende Stadt.

Munich, Bavaria. In the 10th and 11th centuries, monks from the Tegernsee monastery settled on the banks of the River Isar. Today's 1.2 million strong city developed from the monks' settlement »Munichen«.

3

Januar

Theatinerkirche, München: Die Basilika im Stil des italienischen Hochbarock mit einem 71 Meter hohen Kuppelbau wurde 1662 von dem Bologneser Baumeister Agostino Barelli entworfen. Die Rokoko-Fassade gestaltete François de Cuvilliés 100 Jahre später.

Theatinerkirche, Munich. The Italian High Baroque-style basilica with its 71 metre high dome was designed in 1662 by the Bolognese architect Agostino Barelli. The Rococo façade was created 100 years later by François de Cuvilliés.

4

January

St. Bartholomä, Bayern: Nicht weit von Kelheim findet man dieses einsam in den Feldern stehende Kirchlein. Es ist das Gotteshaus der umliegenden Einödhöfe, in dem nur einmal im Jahr, am Bartholomäus-Tag, ein Gottesdienst zelebriert wird.

St Bartholomä, Bavaria. Not far from Kelheim this small church stands alone in the fields. It is the chapel for the surrounding isolated farms. A service is held there only once a year – on Bartholomäus Day.

5

Januar

Marienplatz, München: Der Platz vor dem Rathaus ist seit der Stadtgründung der Mittelpunkt von München. Rechts, mit grünem Dach, steht Münchens älteste Kirche St. Peter, liebevoll »Alter Peter« genannt. Ihre Ursprünge gehen auf das 11. Jh. zurück.

Marienplatz, Munich. The square in front of the town hall has been the centre point of Munich since it was founded. On the right, with the green roof, is Munich's oldest church St Peter's – affectionately known as »Alter Peter« or Old Peter. It dates from the 11th century.

6

January

Burgruine Alerheim, Bayern: Mitten im Ries liegen in einer ausgedehnten Ackerlandschaft auf einer Anhöhe die Reste einer Burg. Während des Dreißigjährigen Kriegs wurde sie zerstört und das nahe gelegene Dorf Alerheim niedergebrannt.

Alerheim castle ruins, Bavaria. In the Ries region, the remains of a castle stand on a banking in open countryside. During the Thirty Years' War, the castle was destroyed and the nearby village of Alerheim was burned down.

7

Januar

Chiemsee, Bayern: Um 772 stiftete Herzog Tassilo das Benediktinerinnenkloster auf der Fraueninsel (auch »Frauenchiemsee« genannt). König Ludwig der Deutsche baute es zur königlichen Pfalz aus. Die autofreie Insel ist nur mit dem Schiff erreichbar.

Chiemsee, Bavaria. Around 772 AD, Duke Tassilo donated the Benedictine Convent on the island Fraueninsel (also known as »Frauenchiemsee«). King Louis the German upgraded it to a royal palatinate. The car-free island can only be reached by boat.

8

January

Chiemsee, Bayern: Während der letzten Eiszeit schoben sich Alpengletscher ins Land und schürften riesige Becken aus. Als vor 10 000 Jahren die Warmzeit begann, sammelte sich darin das Schmelzwasser. So entstanden der Chiemsee und andere Voralpenseen.

Chiemsee, Bavaria. During the last ice age, alpine glaciers swept across the landscape, carving huge hollows into the ground. With the onset of the current interglacial period 10,000 years ago, these hollows collected melt water, leading to the creation of the Chiemsee and other alpine upland lakes.

9

Januar

Heißluftballon bei Kempten, Bayern: Die Käsemetropole Kempten, in der seit 1827 Allgäuer Emmentaler produziert wird, ist die älteste urkundlich erwähnte Stadt Deutschlands. 18 n. Chr. beschrieb der Grieche Strabon die römische Siedlung Cambodunum.

Hot-air balloon near Kempten, Bavaria. The cheese capital Kempten, where Allgäu Emmental cheese has been produced since 1827, is Germany's oldest recorded town. Strabo described the Roman settlement of Cambodunum in the year 18 A.D.

10

January

Wiggensbach, Bayern: Die Pfarrkirche St. Pankratius in Wiggensbach bei Kempten zeigt sich von außen nicht besonders auffällig. Innen lebt sie vom Schmuck der Fresken und der Stuckmarmor-Altäre, die Johann Georg Wirth im Stil des Rokoko gestaltete.

Wiggensbach, Bavaria. St. Pankratius Parish Church in Wiggensbach near Kempten is not particularly remarkable on the outside. Its interior, however, is adorned with frescoes and stucco marble altars, designed in Rococo style by Johann Georg Wirth.

11

Januar

Karlsruhe, Baden-Württemberg: Herzstück der Stadt ist das Markgräfliche Schloss, auf das die Straßen fächerförmig ausgerichtet sind. 1715 ließ Markgraf Karl III. Wilhelm den Prachtbau errichten. Sein heutiges Gesicht erhielt er von 1752 bis 1775.

Karlsruhe, Baden-Württemberg. The margravial palace is the heart of the town, from which the streets fan out. The magnificent building was commissioned in 1715 by the Margrave Karl III Wilhelm. Renovations between 1752 and 1775 rendered the palace as we see it today.

12

January

Befreiungshalle, Bayern: Zur Erinnerung an die siegreichen Schlachten gegen Napoleon in den Befreiungskriegen (1813–1815) ließ Bayernkönig Ludwig I. dieses Nationaldenkmal errichten. Es entstand von 1842 bis 1863 auf dem Michelsberg bei Kelheim.

Hall of Liberation, Bavaria. This national monument was commissioned by King Louis I of Bavaria in celebration of the victorious battles against Napoleon in the Wars of Liberation (1813–1815). It was erected on the Michelsberg near Kelheim between 1842 and 1863.

13

Januar

Der Dom zu Köln, Nordrhein-Westfalen: Sechs Jahrhunderte dauerte es, ehe die größte Kathedrale Deutschlands fertig war – und noch heute sind die Steinmetze der Dombauhütte mit einer fortwährenden Rundumerneuerung des gotischen Riesenbaus beschäftigt.

Cologne Cathedral, North Rhine-Westphalia. It took six hundred years to build Germany's largest cathedral and, even today, the stonemasons of the cathedral workshop work on the continual, ongoing restoration of the gothic masterpiece.

14

January

Lüdenscheid, Nordrhein-Westfalen: Wo heute im Zentrum die evangelische Erlöserkirche steht, erhob sich vom 12. Jh. bis 1823 eine romanische Pfeilerbasilika unter dem seltenen Patrozinium des heiligen Medardus.

Lüdenscheid, North Rhine-Westphalia. In the town centre, where today the protestant Church of our Redeemer stands, a Romanesque pillared basilica towered from the 12th century until 1823 under the rare patronage of Saint Medardus.

15

Januar

Forggensee bei Füssen, Bayern: Das Wechselspiel von Zufrieren und Auftauen zaubert Muster in die Eisschicht auf dem größten künstlichen Gewässer Bayerns. Der Wasserspiegel des Stausees schwankt, was zusätzlich für Bewegung im Eis sorgt.

Forggensee near Füssen, Bavaria. As it freezes and thaws, patterns form in the layer of ice on Bavaria's largest man-made lake. The water level fluctuates, creating additional movement in the ice.

16

January

Sylvensteinspeicher, Bayern: Als die Wasser der Isar, der Dürrach und der Walchen 1959 mit einem vierzig Meter hohen Erdwall aufgestaut wurden, überfluteten sie den kleinen Ort Fall – den Hauptschauplatz von Ludwig Ganghofers Roman »Der Jäger von Fall«.

Sylvenstein Reservoir, Bavaria. When the waters of the Rivers Isar, Dürrach and Walchen were dammed by a forty metre high earth wall in 1959, they flooded the small town of Fall which was the main setting for Ludwig Ganghofer's novel »Der Jäger von Fall« (The Hunter from Fall).

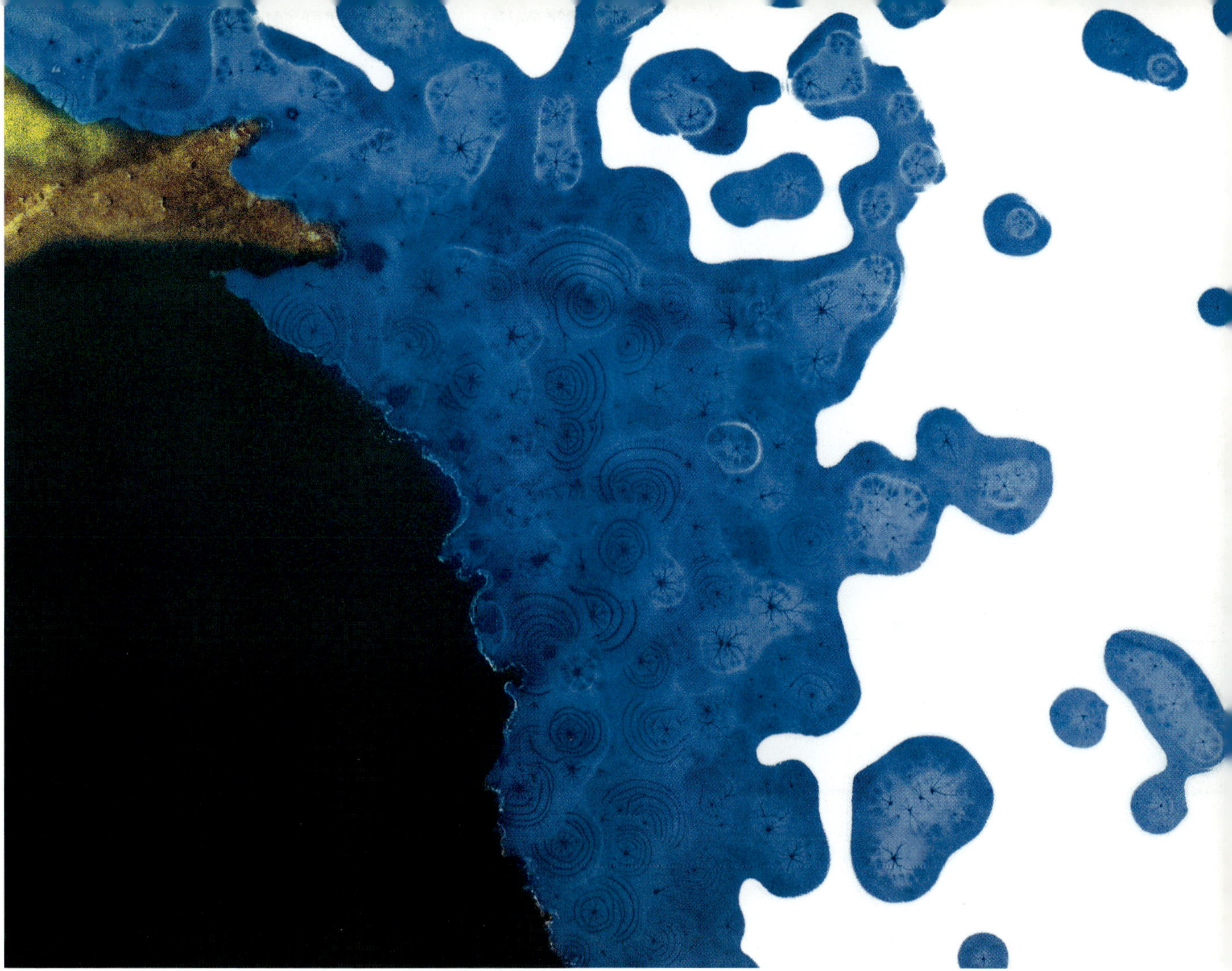

17

Januar

Steigerwald, Bayern: Die bis zu 500 Meter hohen Erhebungen dieses Mittelgebirges zwingen die Regen bringenden Westwinde zum Steigen. Niederschläge sind deshalb häufig, was dem Waldwachstum dienlich ist.

Steiger Forest, Bavaria. This low mountain range, with hills of up to 500 m, causes the rain-bearing west winds to ascend. This leads to frequent rainfall, aiding forest growth.

18

January

Felder bei Wertingen, Bayern: Die Ackerflächen liegen völlig eben auf der schwäbisch-bayerischen Zusam-Platte. Den fruchtbaren Lössboden bliesen Winde in den Jahrhunderten der ausklingenden letzten Eiszeit heran.

Fields near Wertingen, Bavaria. The agricultural land lies flush with the Swabian-Bavarian Zusam plate. The fertile loess soil was carried here on the wind in the centuries at the end of the last ice age.

19

Januar

Benediktinerkloster Neresheim, Baden-Württemberg: In fast himmlischen Höhen liegt die spätbarocke Abteikirche auf dem wolkenumwehten Ulrichsberg. Sie wurde von 1750 bis 1792 nach einem Entwurf des Baumeisters Balthasar Neumann errichtet.

Neresheim Benedictine Monastery, Baden-Württemberg. At nigh-on heavenly altitudes, the late-baroque abbey sits in swirling cloud atop the Ulrichsberg. It was built from 1750 to 1792 based on a design by the master builder Balthasar Neumann.

20

January

Oberallgäu, Baden-Württemberg: Im früheren Albgau lebte der alemannische Stamm der Sueven, der Schwaben. Nach deren Eingliederung ins fränkische Reich begann die Christianisierung. Heute stehen im Allgäu zahlreiche Kapellen, oft einsam in der Flur.

Oberallgäu, Baden-Württemberg. Albgau, as the Allgäu area used to be known, was home to the alemanni tribe of Suebi, or Swabians. After they were incorporated into the Frankish kingdom, Christianisation began. Nowadays numerous isolated chapels are dotted around farmland in the Allgäu.

21

Januar

Felder bei Ochsenfurt, Bayern: Aus dem Maintal geht es steil hinauf auf die Hochfläche der Gäulandschaft, wo jeden Herbst 500 000 Tonnen Zuckerrüben geerntet werden. In der Südzucker AG in Ochsenfurt werden sie seit 1951 weiterverarbeitet.

Fields near Ochsenfurt, Bavaria. From the Main valley the land climbs steeply to the plateau of the Gäu area where every autumn 500,000 tonnes of sugar beet are harvested. The sugar beet has been processed by the company Südzucker AG in Ochsenfurt since 1951.

22

January

Äcker bei Wertingen, Bayern: Nach einer kalten Nacht zeichnet Reif die Strukturen eines Feldes nach. Die Region zwischen Mindelheim und Donauwörth, aus der sich viele flache Moränenhügel erheben, gehört zum »Naturpark Augsburg-Westliche Wälder«.

Fields near Wertingen, Bavaria. After a cold night, frost traces the contours of a field. The region between Mindelheim and Donauwörth, from which many even moraine hills arise, is part of the »Naturpark Augsburg-Westliche Wälder«.

23

Januar

Skiflugschanze bei Oberhof, Thüringen: Nach dem Bau der Eisenbahnstrecke Berlin–Stuttgart 1884 entwickelte sich Oberhof zu Thüringens wichtigstem Wintersportzentrum. Bereits 1906 gab es hier eine Bobbahn und die erste Skiflugschanze.

Ski jump near Oberhof, Thuringia. After the construction of the Berlin–Stuttgart rail line in 1884, Oberhof developed into Thuringia's most important winter sports centre. A bobsleigh run and the first ski jump were here as far back as 1906.

24

January

Skiflugschanze Oberstdorf, Bayern: Die erste Großschanze wurde 1949 im Stillachtal erbaut. Aus Sicherheitsgründen wurde die riesige Holzkonstruktion vor der Weltmeisterschaft 1973 gesprengt und durch eine Spannleichtbeton-Anlage ersetzt.

Oberstdorf ski jump, Bavaria. The first big jump was built in 1949 in the Stillach valley. For safety reasons, the huge wooden construction was demolished before the World Championships in 1973 and replaced with a cantilevered light-weight concrete complex.

25

Januar

Oberstdorf, Bayern: Die Bergwelt um das Nebelhorn (2224 m) und das Fellhorn (2037 m) zählt zu den großen Skigebieten der Alpen. Publikumsmagnet ist alljährlich die Skiflugschanze, auf der ein Springen der Vierschanzentournee stattfindet.

Oberstdorf, Bavaria. The mountainous region of the Nebelhorn (2224 m) and Fellhorn (2037 m) is one of the major ski areas in the Alps. The ski jump, where one of the competitions in the Four Hills Tournament takes place, is a key attraction each year.

26

January

Trudbertkapelle bei Waltrams, Bayern: Die größte der sechs Kapellen im Weitnauer Tal steht am Fuße des Hauchenbergs. Johann Dietrich von Hundbiß soll sie Ende des 17. Jahrhunderts gestiftet haben. Ihr jetziges Gesicht erhielt sie um 1770.

Trudbert Chapel near Waltrams, Bavaria. The largest of six chapels in the Weitnauer valley sits at the foot of the Hauchenberg. Supposedly it was donated by Johann Dietrich von Hundbiß at the end of the 17th century. Its current appearance dates back to 1770.

27

Januar

Simmelsdorf, Bayern:
Im Osten Bayerns hält der Winter häufig recht früh Einzug. Die Fränkische Alb erhebt sich östlich von Nürnberg, wie hier bei Simmelsdorf, auf über 500 Meter Höhe.

Simmelsdorf, Bavaria.
In the east of Bavaria winter often sets in very early. The Franconian Jura rises east of Nuremberg to a height of over 500 metres, as is the case here at Simmelsdorf.

28

January

St. Koloman bei Füssen, Bayern: Wer die Romantische Straße befährt, durchquert auch den »Pfaffenwinkel«, eine Region mit ungezählten Kirchen und Klöstern. Nahe bei Schwangau steht auf freiem Feld seit 1678 die heutige Wallfahrtskirche St. Koloman.

St Koloman near Füssen, Bavaria. Anyone driving the Romantic Road also crosses the »Pfaffenwinkel«, a region with countless churches and monasteries. The Pilgrimage Church St Koloman has stood since 1678 in the middle of a field close to Schwangau.

29

Januar

Hohenloher Ebene, Baden-Württemberg: Die fruchtbare Ebene wird stark agrarisch genutzt. Dank der Leelage hinter Spessart, Odenwald und Schwarzwald herrscht in der Region zwischen Blaufelden und Rothenburg ein bewölkungsarmes, meist sonniges Klima.

Hohenloher Ebene, Baden-Württemberg. This fertile plain is heavily farmed and because it is sheltered from the wind by the Spessart Mountains, the Oden Forest and Black Forest, the region between Blaufelden and Rothenburg has a largely cloudless, sunny climate.

30

January

Winterlinden im Lechtal, Bayern: Man sieht dem stimmungsvollen Bild nicht an, unter welchen Schwierigkeiten es entstand: Mehrere Flugmanöver bei 200 km/h waren nötig, um die Maschine im engen Lechtal in die ideale Position zum Fotografieren zu bringen.

Lime trees in the Lech valley, Bavaria. It's not obvious from this atmospheric photo quite how difficult it was to take. It required several flight manoeuvres at 200 km per hour in the narrow Lech valley to achieve the right position for the shot.

31

Januar

Bei Gundremmingen, Bayern: Über dem bayerischen Voralpengebiet liegt Nebel. Die blaue Linie am Horizont sind die hundert Kilometer entfernten Alpen. Der aufsteigende Dampf kommt aus den Kühltürmen des Kernkraftwerks Gundremmingen bei Günzburg.

Near Gundremmingen, Bavaria. Fog lies over the foothills of the Alps in Bavaria. The blue line on the horizon is the Alps one hundred kilometres away. The rising steam comes from the cooling towers of the Gundremmingen nuclear power plant near Günzburg.

1

Februar

Saulgrub, Bayern: Das Hörnle mit seinen drei Gipfeln – dem Vorderen, Mittleren und Hinteren Hörnle – ist der Hausberg von Saulgrub, einem Kurort, der in fast 900 Meter Höhe am Eingang des Ammertals liegt.

Saulgrub, Bavaria. The Hörnle with its three peaks – the front, middle and rear Hörnle – is the landmark mountain of Saulgrub, a spa resort situated at almost 900 m above sea level at the entrance of the Ammer valley.

2

Februar

Bayerischer Wald: Längs durch das Mittelgebirge verläuft die deutsch-tschechische Grenze. Der eigentliche Bayerische Wald ist der Vordere Wald. Der Hintere Wald galt früher als Teil des Böhmerwaldes, der sich auf tschechischer Seite fortsetzt.

Bavarian Forest. The border between Germany and the Czech Republic runs lengthways through this low mountain range. The actual Bavarian Forest is the »Vordere«, or front, forest. The »Hintere«, or rear, forest used to be part of the Bohemian Forest which continues on the Czech side of the border.

3

February

Rauhe Ebrach, Bayern: Die Keuperstufe im Steigerwald erhebt sich mit einer über 200 Meter hohen Steilwand und flacht nach Osten sanft ab. Dieser Richtung folgt auch die Rauhe Ebrach, die nahe der Keuperstufe entspringt, bis sie in die Regnitz mündet.

Rauhe Ebrach river, Bavaria. The Keuperstufe in the Steiger Forest is a 200 m tall cliff face, which levels out gently towards the east. The Rauhe Ebrach, which springs close to the Keuperstufe, flows in the same direction until it runs into the river Regnitz.

4

Februar

Steigerwald, Bayern: Der Untergrund dieses fränkischen Berglandes besteht aus Keupersandstein, der vor etwa 200 Millionen Jahren abgelagert wurde. Viele alte Bruchsteinhäuser und auch Teile der Nürnberger Kaiserburg wurden damit errichtet.

Steiger Forest, Bavaria. The bedrock of this Franconian highland is Keuper sandstone which was deposited around 200 million years ago. Many old quarry stone houses and parts of Nuremberg's Kaiserburg, or Imperial Castle, were built with it.

5

February

Bayerisches Alpenvorland: Den Naturraum zwischen Donau und Alpen formten die Eiszeiten. In dieser Gegend nahe Landshut entspringen die Kleine und die Große Vils. Alle Bäche und Flüsse strömen nach Nordosten zur Donau hin.

Bavarian Alpenvorland. The landscape between the Danube and the Alps was formed by the ice ages. In this area, near Landshut, the rivers Kleine Vils and Große Vils spring. All streams and rivers flow towards the Danube to the northeast.

6

Februar

Die Rhön, Hessen: In früheren Jahrhunderten arbeiteten die relativ armen Rhöner in der Holz- und Landwirtschaft, als Korbflechter oder Bürstenbinder. Auch heute ist die Rhön mehr Natur- als Wirtschaftsraum. Der Fremdenverkehr spielt eine große Rolle.

The Rhön, Hesse. In centuries gone by, the relatively poor Rhön inhabitants worked in agriculture or forestry, as basket weavers or brush makers. Today the Rhön remains rural, rather than a commercial area. Tourism plays a major role here.

7

February

Die Rhön, Hessen/Thüringen/Bayern: Gleich drei Bundesländer haben Anteil an diesem Mittelgebirge. Die Rhön gilt als »Land der offenen Fernen«: Ihre in weiten Bereichen waldfreien Kuppen eignen sich hervorragend zum Skiwandern und Segelfliegen.

The Rhön in Hesse, Thuringia and Bavaria. This low mountain range spans three federal states in Germany. The Rhön is known as the »place of the wide open spaces«. Its rolling hills are largely forest-free, so ideal for ski-touring and gliding.

8

Februar

Harburg, Bayern: Die größte erhaltene Burg Süddeutschlands, 1093 erstmals urkundlich erwähnt, thront auf einem Felsen der Frankenalb, dort, wo die Wörnitz den Rand des Rieskraters durchbricht, der seine Existenz einem Meteoriteneinschlag verdankt.

Harburg, Bavaria. The largest castle still standing in southern Germany, it was first documented in 1093. It towers on a cliff in the Frankenalb area, where the Wörnitz river breaches the edge of the Ries crater, which was formed by a meteorite impact.

9

February

Donauwörth, Bayern: Die Stadt an der Romantischen Straße war bis zum 17. Jh. unter dem Namen »Schwäbischwerd« bekannt. Ihre Keimzelle war der »Werd«, eine Insel zwischen zwei Armen der Wörnitz, die in Donauwörth in die Donau mündet.

Donauwörth, Bavaria. The town on the Romantic Road was known as »Schwäbischwerd« until the 17th century. The nucleus of the town was the »Werd«, an island between two arms of the River Wörnitz which flows into the Danube in Donauwörth.

10

Februar

Ruine Rothenberg bei Schnaittach, Bayern: 1744 wurde die einst gewaltige Festung einen ganzen Sommer lang von den Truppen Maria Theresias belagert und hielt stand. Im 19. Jh. war sie ein gefürchtetes Gefängnis. Heute sind nur noch Ruinen erhalten.

Rothenberg ruin near Schnaittach, Bavaria. For an entire summer in 1744, the once mighty fortress was besieged by Maria Theresa's troops and withstood them. In the 19th century it was a formidable prison. Today only ruins remain.

11

February

Main bei Randersacker, Bayern: Durch den Ausbau des Mains ging die natürliche Flussaue verloren. Als Ersatz legte man eckige Wasserbecken an. Diese strömungsfreien Laichzonen für Fische frieren im Winter schneller zu als der Fluss selbst.

River Main near Randersacker, Bavaria. With the expansion of the river Main, its natural flood plains were lost. To replace them, angular pools were constructed. There are no currents in these fish spawning ponds, so they freeze over more quickly in winter than the river.

12

Februar

Würzburg, Bayern: In solch winterlichem Gewand zeigt sich die Stadt eher selten. Die geschützte Lage in nur 176 m Höhe in der Beckenlandschaft Mainfrankens, die von Odenwald, Spessart, Rhön und Steigerwald umgeben ist, bewirkt ein mildes Klima.

Würzburg, Bavaria. It is rare to see the city looking so wintery. At an altitude of just 176 m, its protected situation in the Main-Franconian basin, surrounded by the Oden Forest, Spessart Mountains, the Rhön and the Steiger Forest, ensures a mild climate.

13

February

Regensburg, Bayern: Um das Jahr 1250 begannen die Regensburger mit dem Bau ihres Doms. Nahezu 300 Jahre vergingen, bis er – fast – fertiggestellt war; die beiden 105 Meter hohen Türme ließ erst König Ludwig I. von Bayern 1859 bis 1869 hinzufügen.

Regensburg, Bavaria. Work on Regensburg Cathedral began around the year 1250. Almost 300 years later, it was almost completed: the two 105 m high towers were only added on the orders of King Louis I of Bavaria between 1859 and 1869.

14

Februar

Bei Zittau, Sachsen: Deutschlands kleinstes Mittelgebirge, das Zittauer Gebirge im südöstlichsten Zipfel von Sachsen, besteht vorwiegend aus Sandstein und geht in das in Tschechien gelegene Lausitzer Gebirge über.

Near Zittau, Saxony. The Zittau hills, Germany's smallest low mountain range at the south-easternmost point of Saxony, are made mainly of sandstone and give way to the Lausitz hills of the Czech Republic.

15

February

Nürnberg, Bayern: Das Wahrzeichen der Stadt ist die Kaiserburg. Sie wurde im 11. Jh. unter Kaiser Heinrich III. begonnen; nach der Zerstörung im Zweiten Weltkrieg bauten die Bürger sie innerhalb von zwei Jahrzehnten wieder auf.

Nuremberg, Bavaria. The Kaiserburg, or Imperial Castle, is the emblem of the city. Its construction began in the 11th century under Emperor Henry III. Following its destruction in the Second World War, Nuremberg's citizens rebuilt it within two decades.

16

Februar

Alte Mainbrücke in Würzburg, Bayern: Nachdem Eisgang die erste, 1133 errichtete Steinbrücke über den Main zerstört hatte, baute man im 15. Jh. eine neue, deren Pfeiler noch heute stehen. Unter der Brücke befinden sich eine Schleuse und ein E-Werk.

Alte Mainbrücke in Würzburg, Bavaria. After ice drift destroyed the first stone bridge over the Main river, which dated back to 1133, a new bridge was constructed in the 15th century, whose pillars are still standing today. A lock and a power station are situated below the bridge.

17

February

Heidelberg, Baden-Württemberg: Bis zu seiner Sprengung im Pfälzischen Erbfolgekrieg war das Heidelberger Schloss die Residenz der Pfälzer Kurfürsten. Obwohl es heute in vielen Teilen nur noch als Ruine besteht, zieht es Touristen aus aller Welt an.

Heidelberg, Baden-Württemberg. Until its demolition during the War of the Grand Alliance, the Palace of Heidelberg was the seat of the Palatine electors. Although it is largely a ruin today, it attracts tourists from all over the world.

18

Februar

Wallfahrtskirche zur Heiligen Dreifaltigkeit bei Waldsassen, Bayern: Die sogenannte Kappel ist eine architektonische Umsetzung des Dreieinigkeitsgedankens. Der 1685–1689 errichtete Rundbau wird in fast allen Elementen von der Zahl Drei beherrscht.

Pilgrimage Church of the Holy Trinity near Waldsassen, Bavaria. The »Kappel«, as it is known, is an architectural realisation of the notion of the Holy Trinity. The rotunda, which was constructed between 1685 and 1689, is dominated by the number three in nearly every detail.

19

February

Wallfahrtskirche St. Wolfgang bei Landshut, Bayern: Während einer Reise soll der Regensburger Bischof Wolfgang hier eine Rast eingelegt haben. An der Stelle, wo er der Legende nach einen Abdruck im Stein hinterließ, errichtete man später die Kirche.

St. Wolfgang Pilgrimage Church near Landshut, Bavaria. According to legend, Bishop Wolfgang of Regensburg rested here on a journey. The church was later erected on the spot where he supposedly left an impression in the rock.

20

Februar

Versetalsperre, Nordrhein-Westfalen: Von Attendorn nach Lüdenscheid führt eine landschaftlich reizvolle Nebenstrecke durch das Sauerland, die am Westufer der Versetalsperre mittels einer Steinbrücke eine Bucht überquert.

Versetalsperre reservoir, North Rhine-Westphalia. From Attendorn to Lüdenscheid, an alternative route through the Sauerland region delivers beautiful scenery. On the west bank of the Versetalsperre, this route crosses a bay via a stone bridge.

21

February

Elbe-Havel-Kanal, Sachsen-Anhalt: Die 56 km lange Wasserstraße führt ab Magdeburg den von Hannover kommenden Mittellandkanal nach Osten fort. Das Bild zeigt die Einmündung in die Elbe bei Niegripp.

The Elbe-Havel Canal, Saxony Anhalt. From Magdeburg, the 56 km long waterway continues the Mittelland Canal coming eastwards from Hanover. The picture shows its confluence with the River Elbe near Niegripp.

22

Februar

Vereiste Oberfläche des Altmühlsees, Bayern: Der in einem weiten, flachen Wiesengrund geschaffene Stausee wird von Hochwassern der Altmühl gespeist. Die über einen Quadratkilometer große Insel- und Flachwasserzone ist ein Vogelschutzgebiet.

Frozen surface of the Altmühlsee, Bavaria. The reservoir, which lies in a vast, flat grassland area, collects flood water from the river Altmühl. With its islands and shallow water, it has an area of over one square kilometre and is a bird sanctuary.

23

February

Braunkohleabbau bei Frechen, Nordrhein-Westfalen: Deutschland ist der größte Braunkohleproduzent weltweit. Da sich der wertvolle Rohstoff in geringen Tiefen befindet, wird er im Tagebau gewonnen. Er dient vor allem zur Energieerzeugung.

Brown coal mining near Frechen, North Rhine-Westphalia. Germany is the largest supplier of brown coal worldwide. This valuable natural resource lies close to the surface and is recovered using opencast mining. It is used largely for generating energy.

24

Februar

Niedersonthofner See, Bayern: Wie alle Voralpenseen ist auch dieser Allgäuer See stark verlandet. Die Sommerresidenz, die Fürstabt Roman Giel von Gielsberg um 1650 auf einer Insel erbauen ließ, liegt heute weitab vom Ufer auf dem Festland.

Niedersonthofner Lake, Bavaria. This Allgäu lake has dried up quite dramatically, as have all the lakes in the foothills of the Alps. The summer residence, which Prince Abbott Roman Giel von Gielsberg had built on an island in 1650, today lies on the mainland, some distance from the water's edge.

25

February

Auwälder bei Höchstädt, Bayern: Die winterstarren Fischteiche lassen nicht ahnen, dass hier am 13.8. 1704 ein schlimmes Gemetzel stattfand: In der Schlacht bei Höchstädt vernichteten österreichisch-englische Truppen ein bayerisch-französisches Heer.

Lowland forest near Höchstädt, Bavaria. Looking at the frozen fish-ponds, you'd never guess this was the site of a bloody massacre on the 13th August 1704. At the Battle of Blenheim, Austro-English troops destroyed a Franco-Bavarian army.

26

Februar

Kapelle bei Neumarkt, Bayern: Zahlreiche Klöster, Wallfahrtskapellen und Dorfkirchen zeugen von der Religiosität, die das Landschaftsbild und die Menschen in der Oberpfalz über Jahrhunderte hinweg geprägt hat.

Chapel near Neumarkt, Bavaria. Numerous monasteries, pilgrimage chapels and village churches attest to the religiousness that, for centuries, has shaped both landscape and people of the Upper Palatinate.

27

February

Würzburg, Bayern: Auf halber Höhe am Steilhang des Nikolausbergs steht die Wallfahrtskirche Mariä Heimsuchung – im Volksmund »Käppele« genannt. Hinauf führt ein Kreuzweg mit 265 Stufen, den 65 lebensgroße Figuren säumen.

Würzburg, Bavaria. The pilgrimage church of Mariä Heimsuchung, commonly known as the »Käppele«, stands half way up the steep face of the Nikolaus mountain. A way of the cross with 265 steps, edged with 65 life-size figures, leads up to the chapel.

28

Februar

Zschopau, Sachsen: Von Oberwiesenthal aus kann man mit der Schwebebahn auf den 1214 m hohen Fichtelberg fahren. Wintervergnügen im Tal bietet eine Schlittenfahrt an der Zschopau, die am Fichtelberg entspringt und der Elbe zuströmt.

Zschopau, Saxony. From Oberwiesenthal you can take a cable car up the 1214 m high Fichtelberg. Winter fun in the valley can be had sledging by the Zschopau river, which rises at the Fichtelberg and flows towards the Elbe.

29

February

Escherndorf, Bayern: Die Weinberge des fränkischen Winzerortes an der Mainschleife fangen mit ihrer Südostausrichtung ideal die Sonnenkraft ein. Silvaner und Riesling von der Spitzenlage »Escherndorfer Lump« werden von Weinkennern hoch geschätzt.

Escherndorf, Bavaria. The south-east facing vineyards of the Franconian winegrowing town on the bend in the River Main are ideal for catching the sun's rays. Silvaner and Riesling from the premium location of the »Escherndorfer Lump« are highly regarded by wine connoisseurs.

1

März

Alte Sorge, Schleswig-Holstein: Durch Vermoorungen und Überschlickungen mit Gezeitensedimenten entwickelte sich die Flusslandschaft Eider-Treene-Sorge zu einem Niederungsgebiet, in dem die Flüsse kaum Strömung haben und starke Schlingen ausbilden.

Alte Sorge, Schleswig-Holstein. Due to swamp formation and silt deposits washed up on the tide, the landscape by the Eider, Treene and Sorge rivers has developed into a floodplain. The rivers have very little current and form distinct loops.

2

March

Helgoland, Schleswig-Holstein: Als einzige Inseln in der südlichen Nordsee bestehen Helgoland und die Nachbarinsel Düne aus festem Gestein. Bis zu sechzig Meter hoch ragt der geschichtete Buntsandstein aus dem Wasser empor.

Helgoland, Schleswig-Holstein. Heligoland and the neighbouring island of Düne are the only islands in the southern North Sea made of solid rock. The layered red sandstone towers up to sixty metres out of the water.

3

März

Dithmarschen, Schleswig-Holstein: Die geringe Wassertiefe in der Meldorfer Bucht erfordert von den Schiffsführern präzises Navigieren. Von der breiten Wasserrinne der »Piep« führt ein viel schmalerer Arm, das »Kronenloch«, zum Neuen Meldorfer Hafen.

Dithmarschen, Schleswig-Holstein. The shallow waters of Meldorf Bight demand precise navigational skills from skippers. From the wide gully, known as the »Piep«, a much narrower arm, known as the »Kronenloch«, leads to the new harbour in Meldorf.

4

March

Gröde-Appelland, Schleswig-Holstein: Die Hallig Gröde ist eine von zehn Halligen im Nordfriesischen Wattenmeer. Eine Sturmflut verband sie mit der Hallig Appelland zu einer jetzt 280 Hektar großen Insel.

Gröde-Appelland, Schleswig-Holstein. The islet Gröde is one of ten islets in the North Frisian Wadden Sea. A storm tide connected it to the islet Appelland, creating one island of 280 hectares.

5

März

Puttgarden, Schleswig-Holstein: Die kürzeste Eisenbahn- und Straßenverbindung nach Skandinavien führt über die Insel Fehmarn. Vom Fährhafen von Puttgarden pendeln rund um die Uhr Fährschiffe nach Rødbyhavn auf der dänischen Insel Lolland und zurück.

Puttgarden, Schleswig-Holstein. The most direct rail and road route to Scandinavia goes via the island of Fehmarn. From Puttgarden ferry terminal, ferries sail round the clock to and from Rødbyhavn on the Danish island of Lolland.

6

March

Kiel, Schleswig-Holstein: Die Kieler Howaldtswerke-Deutsche Werft AG ist die größte deutsche Werft. Über 3000 Angestellte bauen dort Handels- und Marineschiffe. Am gegenüberliegenden Schwedenkai legen die Fährschiffe der Stena-Linie an.

Kiel, Schleswig-Holstein. Kiel's Howaldtswerke-Deutsche Werft AG is the largest German shipyard. With over 3000 employees, it builds commercial and naval ships. Stena Line ferries dock at the Sweden Quay opposite.

7

März

Hafenanlage von Bremerhaven: Als im 19. Jh. der Hafen von Bremen zu versanden drohte, kaufte Bürgermeister Johann Smidt an der Mündung von Weser und Geeste 381 Morgen Land. Hier legte er – 65 Kilometer von Bremen entfernt – den »Bremer Haven« an.

Bremerhaven harbour. When Bremen's port risked silting up in the 19th century, mayor Johann Smidt bought 381 morgens of land on the estuary mouth of the Weser and Geeste rivers. He had the »Bremer Haven« or Port of Bremen constructed here, some 65 kilometres away from the actual city of Bremen.

8

March

Wangerooge, Niedersachsen: 20 Jahre lang patrouillierte Heinz Kipp mit seinem Wasserflugzeug an der Nordseeküste. Er war flugtechnischer Leiter des Vereins Küstenwache Deutsche Nordsee, der zum Schutz der Küstenregion vor Verschmutzung gegründet wurde.

Wangerooge, Lower Saxony. For 20 years, Heinz Kipp patrolled the North Sea coast with his seaplane. He was flight director of the association German North Sea Coastal Watch, which was formed to protect the coastal area from pollution.

9

März

Föhr, Schleswig-Holstein: Die Nordfriesische Insel ist vom offenen Meer durch Sylt und Amrum abgeschirmt; die typische Nordseebrandung fehlt hier. Anders als die Nachbarinseln wird Föhr von Marschwiesen und Feldern statt von Strand und Dünen geprägt.

Föhr, Schleswig-Holstein. This North Friesian island is sheltered from the open sea, and the typical North Sea surge, by the islands of Sylt and Amrum. In contrast to its neighbouring islands, Föhr is characterised by fields and fens rather than beaches and dunes.

10

March

Elbhafen von Brunsbüttel, Schleswig-Holstein: Ein Bugsierkutter hilft einem Küstenmotorschiff beim Wenden. Seit 1967 bietet der Elbhafen Schiffen mit einem Tiefgang von bis zu 13 Metern alle notwendigen Umschlagmöglichkeiten.

The port of Brunsbüttel on the Elbe, Schleswig-Holstein. A tug helps a coaster to turn. The port has been providing comprehensive handling services to ships with a draught of up to 13 metres.

11

März

Scharhörn, Niedersachsen: Die Insel entstand ab 1925, als sich im Hamburgischen Wattenmeer kleine Dünen angehäuft hatten. Durch Wellen und Wind getrieben wandert sie nach Südosten. Was auf der Luvseite abgetragen wird, setzt sich auf Lee an.

Scharhörn, Lower Saxony. The island emerged from 1925 onwards, when small dunes accumulated in the Hamburg Wadden Sea. Driven by wind and the waves, it's moving towards the south east. Erosion on the windward side of the island resettles on the lee side.

12

March

Wattenmeer, Niedersachsen: Zwischen den Trichtermündungen der Ems und der Elbe erstreckt sich der Nationalpark Niedersächsisches Wattenmeer. Die Sandbänke sind ein idealer Lebensraum für Seehunde, die hier im Sommer ihren Nachwuchs zur Welt bringen.

The Wadden Sea, Lower Saxony. The Wadden Sea National Park of Lower Saxony lies between the estuaries of the Rivers Ems and Elbe. The sandbanks are an ideal habitat for seals, which bear their young here in summer.

13

März

Mündung der Peene, Mecklenburg-Vorpommern: Entlang des Flusslaufs der Peene erstreckt sich das größte in sich geschlossene Niedermoorgebiet Mitteleuropas. Es ist eines der letzten noch weitgehend intakten Erbstücke der Eiszeit.

Peene estuary, Mecklenburg-Western Pomerania. The largest self-contained fen area of central Europe runs along the course of the river Peene. It is one of the last remaining largely intact legacies of the ice age.

14

March

Fehmarn, Schleswig-Holstein: Von der Südwestspitze der Insel aus wächst der Krummsteert, ein sogenannter Nehrungshaken, in die Orther Bucht hinein. Durch Strömungen, die Sand und Geröll mit sich führen, vergrößert sich das Naturschutzgebiet ständig.

Fehmarn, Schleswig-Holstein. From the south-western tip of the island, the Krummsteert spit protrudes into Orth Bay. This nature reserve is growing gradually bigger due to sand and rubble carried in on the tide.

15

März

Wismarbucht, Mecklenburg-Vorpommern: Meereswellen werden durch Wind ausgelöst; ihre Ausprägung hängt von Windstärke, Küstenform und Wassertiefe ab. Als Dünung – wie hier im Bild – bezeichnet man kleine Wellen, die nach Abflauen des Windes auslaufen.

Wismar Bay, Mecklenburg-Western Pomerania. Waves are triggered by the wind and their magnitude depends on wind strength, the contour of the coast and the depth of the water. Groundswell – as shown here – is the name given to small waves which peter out when the wind abates.

16

March

Rügen, Mecklenburg-Vorpommern: Die Kreidefelsen zwischen Lohme und Sassnitz ragen über hundert Meter aus der Ostsee auf. Sie sind Teil des Nationalparks Jasmund, der im Nordosten der größten und wohl auch schönsten deutschen Insel liegt.

Rügen, Mecklenburg-Western Pomerania. The chalk cliffs between the towns of Lohme and Sassnitz tower over 100 metres out of the Baltic Sea. They are part of the Jasmund National Park, situated in the north-east of Germany's largest and, arguably, most beautiful island.

17

März

Dollart, Niedersachsen: Nachdem sie das nach ihr benannte Emsland durchflossen hat, mündet die Ems in den Dollart. Diese Nordseebucht entstand durch mehrere große Sturmfluten seit dem 14. Jahrhundert.

Dollart, Lower Saxony. After the River Ems has traversed the Emsland region named after it, it flows into Dollart bay. This North Sea bay was created by several powerful storm tides since the 14th century.

18

March

Stade, Niedersachsen: Der Ortsteil Bützfleth ist Standort einer Industrieanlage, die Aluminiumoxid herstellt. Als Produktionsabfall bei der Bauxitverarbeitung bleibt eisenhaltiges Wasser übrig. In einem Absetzbecken kann der Rotschlamm sedimentieren.

Stade, Lower Saxony. The Bützfleth area of Stade is the site of an industrial plant producing aluminium oxide. Processing bauxite generates ferrous waste water. A settling tank allows the red sludge to sediment.

19

März

Uelzen, Niedersachsen: Der wilhelminische Bahnhof wurde im Rahmen eines Projekts zur EXPO 2000 in Hannover von dem Künstler Friedensreich Hundertwasser umgestaltet. Auf dem Dach installierte man die größte Fotovoltaikanlage Niedersachsens.

Uelzen, Lower Saxony. The Wilhelmine railway station was redesigned by the artist Friedensreich Hundertwasser for the EXPO 2000 in Hanover. The largest electricity-generating solar panel unit in Lower Saxony is installed on the roof.

20

March

Papenburg, Niedersachsen: Seit über 200 Jahren baut die Meyer-Werft Schiffe, früher aus Holz, seit 1874 aus Eisen. Neben Gastankern und Tiertransportern sind luxuriöse Kreuzfahrt- und Fährschiffe die Spezialität des Familienunternehmens.

Papenburg, Lower Saxony. The Meyer shipyard has been building ships for over 200 years, previously from wood but since 1874 from iron. As well as gas tankers and animal freight ships, luxury liners and ferries are the specialism of this family concern.

21

März

Fernsehturm, Berlin: Ein unübersehbares Wahrzeichen Berlins ist der 368 Meter hohe »Telespargel« auf dem Alexanderplatz. In 207 Meter Höhe befindet sich ein drehbares Café, das einen Rundblick mit bis zu vierzig Kilometer Sichtweite bietet.

Television tower, Berlin. It's hard to miss this 368 m high iconic symbol of Berlin, dubbed the »TV asparagus«, on Alexanderplatz. 207 m up there is a revolving café which provides a panoramic view with visibility of up to 40 km.

22

March

Zitadelle Spandau, Berlin: Die von der Havel umflossene Zitadelle entstand im 16. Jh. auf den Grundmauern der schon vorhandenen Burganlage. Der Festungsbau galt als uneinnehmbar. Später diente die Zitadelle als Staatsgefängnis.

Zitadelle Spandau, Berlin. Dating back to the 16th century, the fortress – surrounded by the River Havel – was built on the foundations of the existing castle. The fortress was considered to be impenetrable and later became a state prison.

23

März

Jänschwalde, Brandenburg: Die Schaufelradbagger im Braunkohletagebaugebiet fressen sich immer weiter durch die Lausitzer Landschaft. Tonnenweise fördern sie Kohle zutage, lassen aber dabei ganze Landstriche und sogar Dörfer verschwinden.

Jänschwalde, Brandenburg. The bucket-wheel excavators in this brown coal open-cast mining area devour more and more of the Lausitz countryside. They unearth the coal by the tonne, destroying whole swathes of countryside and even villages in the process.

24

March

Oschersleben, Sachsen-Anhalt: Inmitten der landwirtschaftlich genutzten Magdeburger Börde liegt die Formel-1-taugliche Rennstrecke Motopark Oschersleben. Erste Pläne gab es bereits nach dem Zerfall der DDR. Am 25. Juli 1997 wurde die Anlage eröffnet.

Oschersleben, Saxony-Anhalt. The Motopark Oschersleben race track, which is suitable for Formula 1, sits amidst the farmland of the »Magdeburger Börde«. Initial plans for its construction were laid after the collapse of the GDR and the complex was opened on 25th July 1997.

25

März

Frankfurt/Oder, Brandenburg: Den deutsch-polnischen Grenzübergang Frankfurt/Oder–Swiecko passieren jährlich eine Million Lkws. Vor dem Zollterminal, auf einer Parkfläche mit 900 Stellplätzen, warten die Lastzüge auf ihre Abfertigung.

Frankfurt (Oder), Brandenburg. A million lorries a year cross the German-Polish border at Frankfurt (Oder)–Swiecko. In front of the customs building, the juggernauts await customs clearance in a holding area with 900 spaces.

26

March

Aschersleben, Sachsen-Anhalt: Die landwirtschaftlichen Flächen im Landkreis Aschersleben-Staßfurt weisen die höchsten Bodenwertzahlen in Deutschland auf. Zuckerrüben, Getreide, Kartoffeln und Gewürze, vor allem Majoran, gedeihen auf den Feldern.

Aschersleben, Saxony-Anhalt. The agricultural land in the district of Aschersleben-Staßfurt is the most fertile soil in Germany. Sugar beet, grain, potatoes and spices – in particular marjoram – thrive here.

27

März

Langenberg, Nordrhein-Westfalen: Anlässlich des Großprojekts »Tuchfühlung II: Körperkonturen«, das der Kulturverein Langenberg im Jahr 2000 initiierte, schuf der Münchner Land-Art-Künstler Heinrich Bunzel diese 120 Meter große Figur.

Langenberg, North Rhine-Westphalia. As part of the project »Tuchfühlung II: Körperkonturen«, staged by the cultural association of Langenberg in 2000, the Munich »Land Art« artist Heinrich Bunzel sculpted this 120 m tall figure.

28

March

Industriegebiet von Ludwigshafen, Rheinland-Pfalz: Die Stadt wurde 1853 am Rheinufer gegenüber der Residenzstadt Mannheim gegründet. Sie trägt den Namen von Bayernkönig Ludwig I. Heute ist sie geprägt von der Industrie, insbesondere der chemischen.

The industrial area of Ludwigshafen, Rhineland-Palatinate. The city was founded in 1853 on the banks of the Rhine, across from the royal city of Mannheim. Ludwigshafen is named after the king of Bavaria, Louis I. Today it is a centre of industry, more specifically the chemical industry.

29

März

Steigerwald, Bayern: Rötlich färbt die untergehende Sonne den Himmel. Beim flachwinkligen Hineinscheinen in die Atmosphäre werden die blauen Lichtanteile durch Luftpartikel gestreut. Nur das langwellige rote Licht erreicht das Auge des Betrachters.

Steiger Forest, Bavaria. The sky takes on the reddish tone of the sinking sun. When the setting sun shines into the atmosphere, the blue rays are dispersed by the air's components. Only long wave red light rays can be seen by the human eye.

30

March

Steigerwald, Bayern: Das Süddeutsche Schichtstufenland zwischen Rhön und Donau, zu dem auch der Steigerwald gehört, besteht aus Sedimentgesteinen. Durch Verwitterung und Abtragung bildeten sich typische Stufen und darauf ein »steigender Wald«.

Steiger Forest, Bavaria. The southern German escarpment between the Rhön area and the Danube, of which the Steiger Forest is part, is made up of sedimentary rock. Weather and erosion led to the creation of the typical strata, and upon that, a »steigender« or »ascending« forest.

31

März

Wörnitz, Bayern: Beim Flug über das Ries fällt die südwärts fließende Wörnitz ins Auge. Sie kann gewaltige Wassermassen mit sich führen, überschwemmt dann weite Wiesenflächen und setzt den Ort Harburg meterhoch unter Wasser.

River Wörnitz, Bavaria. When flying over the Ries area, the south-flowing Wörnitz catches the eye. It can carry a huge amount of water and when it does, submerges vast grassland areas and causes major flooding in the town of Harburg.

1

April

Main, Bayern: Sinn und Saale hat der Main in Gemünden bereits aufgenommen, danach fließt er in seinem unsteten Verlauf wieder einmal nach Südwesten. Die ICE-Bahntrasse folgt dem Maintal Richtung Lohr.

River Main, Bavaria. The Main has already absorbed the Sinn and Saale rivers in Gemünden. After that it continues its erratic course, once again to the south west. The ICE high speed train route follows the Main valley towards Lohr.

2

April

Neckartal im Odenwald, Baden-Württemberg: Im Westen, wo der Neckar glänzt, liegt die Universitätsstadt Heidelberg. Sie gilt als eine der Wiegen der deutschen Romantik. Kaum weniger romantisch ist der Odenwald mit seinen vielen Burgen und Klöstern.

Necker valley in the Oden Forest, Baden-Württemberg. The university town of Heidelberg lies to the west, by the glistening Neckar river. The town is considered to be one of the cradles of German romanticism. The Oden Forest is scarcely any less romantic with its many castles and monasteries.

3

April

Schwanberg, Bayern: Auf dem sagenumwobenen Berg im Steigerwald bestand bereits um 7000 v. Chr. eine ständige Siedlung. Die Kelten legten eine Fliehburg an und brachten ihrer Göttin Svana Opfer dar; die Germanen beteten dort die Schwanenjungfrauen an.

Schwanberg, Bavaria. A permanent settlement on the legendary mountain in the Steiger Forest existed as far back as 7000 B.C. The Celts built a refuge there and brought offerings to their Goddess Svana, while the Germanic tribes worshipped mythical Swan Maidens here.

4

April

Freiburg im Breisgau, Baden-Württemberg: Auf 278 Meter über dem Meeresspiegel im Oberrheingraben gelegen, erlebt die Universitätsstadt ein äußerst günstiges Klima. Doch unmittelbar dahinter beginnt die regenreiche, herbe Region des Südschwarzwalds.

Freiburg in the Breisgau region, Baden-Württemberg. At 278 m above sea level in the Upper-Rhine rift, the university town enjoys an extremely favourable climate. Yet directly behind it lies the harsh, rainy region of the southern Black Forest.

5

April

Gerchsheim, Baden-Württemberg: Die Autobahn Würzburg–Ulm und die Romantische Straße, die an dem Dorf vorbeiführen, beeinflussen kaum seine landwirtschaftliche Prägung. Ringsum in der Gäulandschaft liegt seit Jahrtausenden fruchtbarer Lössboden.

Gerchsheim, Baden-Württemberg. The motorway from Würzburg to Ulm and the Romantic Road, which run past this village, have little impact on its agricultural character. All over the Gäulandschaft area, fertile loess soil has been present for thousands of years.

6

April

Frankfurt am Main: Vom Taunus her kommend, wird deutlich, warum man die hessische Metropole »Mainhattan« nennt. Bürotürme von Banken und Versicherungen ragen hoch in den Himmel; der Sitz der Commerzbank (298 m) ist das höchste Bürogebäude Europas.

Frankfurt am Main. Approaching from the Taunus region, it's obvious why the Hessian city is known as »Mainhatten«. Looming skyscrapers are home to banks and insurance companies. The Commerzbank tower is the tallest office building in Europe at 298 m.

7

April

Lübeck, Schleswig-Holstein: 1143 errichtete Graf Adolf von Schauenburg eine Kaufmannssiedlung, umgeben von den Flüssen Wakenitz und Trave. Ihr Name Lubeke stammt vom slawischen Liubice (die Schöne). Seit dem 13. Jh. ist Lübeck »Hansestadt«.

Lübeck, Schleswig-Holstein. In 1143, Count Adolf von Schauenburg established a merchants' colony, encircled by the rivers Wakenitz and Trave. Its name Lubeke derives from the Slavic »Liubice«, meaning beautiful one. Lubeck has been a »Hanseatic City« since the 13th century.

8

April

Wilhelmshaven, Niedersachsen: Der Jadebusen und die Trichtermündung der Jade erhielten ihre Form erst im Mittelalter durch gewaltige Sturmfluten. Am Ende der Bucht liegt der Ölhafen von Wilhelmshaven, in dem auch Supertanker anlegen können.

Wilhelmshaven, Lower Saxony. Jade bay and estuary were only formed in the middle ages by huge storm tides. Wilhelmshaven's oil port, suitable also for very large crude carriers, is sited at the edge of the bay.

9

April

Maschen, Niedersachsen: Der Rangierbahnhof Maschen bei Hamburg ist seit 1980 in Betrieb. Er wurde damals als technisches Wunder bezeichnet und war der größte und modernste Rangierbahnhof Europas.

Maschen, Lower Saxony. The marshalling yard Maschen, near Hamburg, has been operating since 1980. At that stage it was considered to be a technological marvel and was the largest and most modern marshalling yard in Europe.

10

April

Esterweger Dose, Niedersachsen: Bevor die Behörden 1959 die Genehmigung zum Abtorfen erteilten, war die Esterweger Dose östlich von Papenburg das größte zusammenhängende Hochmoorgebiet Mitteleuropas. Heute steht ein Teil unter Naturschutz.

Esterweger Dose, Lower Saxony. Before the authorities gave the green light for peat digging there in 1959, the Esterweger Dose to the east of Papenburg was the largest continuous area of upland moor in central Europe. Today part of it is a conservation area.

11

April

Kurhaus Juist, Niedersachsen: Das Strandhotel hat schon viele Stürme überstanden, auch den von 1906, als die Nordsee ins Parterre eindrang und die Wandelhalle verwüstete. Zum Schutz baute man 1911 eine Strandmauer.

Kurhaus Juist, Lower Saxony. The seaside hotel has survived many storms, including one in 1906 when the North Sea flooded the ground floor and destroyed the lobby. In 1911, a protective beach wall was constructed.

12

April

Nordseeküste, Schleswig-Holstein: Die Meldorfer Bucht von Büsum bis Friedrichskoogspitze gehört zum Nationalpark Schleswig-Holsteinisches Wattenmeer. Ein Deich schützt das Land vor Überschwemmung bei Spring- und Sturmfluten.

North Sea coast, Schleswig-Holstein. Meldorf Bight from Büsum to Friedrichskoogspitze is part of the Schleswig-Holstein Wadden Sea National Park. A dyke protects the mainland from spring tides and storm tides.

13

April

Friedrichskoog, Schleswig-Holstein: Der Naturraum Junge Marsch ist durch Sedimentation aus der Wattenküste der Nordsee entstanden. Dieser natürliche Vorgang wird von den Dithmarschern gefördert: Dazu legen sie niedrige Dämme, die Lahnungen, an.

Friedrichskoog, Schleswig-Holstein. As an area of unspoiled nature, the Junge Marsch was created by sedimentation from the Wadden coast of the North Sea. This natural process is boosted in Dithmarschen by the construction of low dams, or breakwaters.

14

April

Laboe, Schleswig-Holstein: Rund um die Kieler Förde ist der Segelsport weit verbreitet. An der Außenförde im Stadtteil Schilksee befindet sich der Olympiahafen von 1972. Gegenüber, im Hafen von Laboe, haben Freizeitboote und ein Fischkutter angelegt.

Laboe, Schleswig-Holstein. Sailing is very popular around the Firth of Kiel. Schilksee, on the mouth of the firth, is home to the 1972 Olympic marina. Across the water, in the harbour of Laboe, leisure boats and a fishing cutter are docked.

15

April

Wilhelmshaven, Niedersachsen: Zum einzigen deutschen Tiefwasserhafen gehört auch der einige Kilometer meerwärts gelegene Ölhafen. 1869 weihte Wilhelm I. von Preußen einen Kriegsmarinehafen ein und gab der zeitgleich entstandenen Siedlung seinen Namen.

Wilhelmshaven, Lower Saxony. The oil port, which lies a few kilometres seawards, is part of Germany's only deep-water harbour. In 1869, William I of Prussia inaugurated a naval port, giving his name to the town that was founded at the same time.

16

April

Große Kirr, Mecklenburg-Vorpommern: Die Vogelinsel ist Teil des Nationalparks Vorpommersche Boddenlandschaft. Dort findet sich noch ursprüngliches Salzgrasland mit zahlreichen Prielen und Salzpfannen.

Große Kirr, Mecklenburg-Western Pomerania. The bird island belongs to the Western Pomeranian Bodden National Park. Original salt-marsh is found there, with its numerous tidal creeks and salt pans.

17

April

[W]ühle bei Nerdin, Mecklenburg-Vorpommern: Das Küstentiefland ist klima[t]isch ausgeglichener als das Binnenland, die Erwärmung im Frühjahr setzt [a]llerdings etwas später ein. [D]ie Windmühle bei Nerdin half früher beim Entwässern der feuchten Böden.

Windmill near Nerdin, Mecklenburg-Western Pomerania. The coastal lowlands have a more stable climate than inland, although the springtime rise in temperatures sets in a little later. The windmill [n]ear Nerdin used to help drain the boggy ground.

18

April

Koos, Mecklenburg-Vorpommern: Innerhalb des Greifswalder Boddens bildet sich im Naturschutzgebiet der Halbinsel eine Binnennehrung – eine schmale Sandbank. Die Strömung nimmt fortwährend Sand mit und lagert ihn wenige Meter weiter wieder ab.

Koos, Mecklenburg-Western Pomerania. Within the Greifswalder Bodden, a narrow sandbank forms a kind of spit in the peninsula's conservation area. The tide continually carries in sand and deposits it a few metres further on.

19

April

Bei Anklam, Mecklenburg-Vorpommern: Bevor die Peene in das Oderhaff mündet, staut sich ihr Wasser im Peenetalmoor, dem größten zusammenhängenden Niedermoorgebiet Deutschlands. Hier verfremdet die Reflexion des Abendrots die Uferkonturen.

Near Anklam, Mecklenburg-Western Pomerania. Before the river Peene flows into the Oder lagoon, its water accumulates on the Peenetalmoor, the largest continuous area of lowland moor in Germany. Here the reflection of the setting sun distorts the contours of the shore.

20

April

Felder bei Greifswald, Mecklenburg-Vorpommern
Die agrarischen Böden hier zählen nicht zu den besten. Eiszeitgletscher verursachten eine Entkalkung, eine Ausspülung des Feinmaterials und eine Überdeckung des Untergrunds mit Flugsand oder Sandlöss.

Fields near Greifswald, Mecklenburg-Western Pomerania. The agrarian land here is far from the best. Ice age glaciers decalcified the soil, washed away finer materials and covered the subsoil with wind-borne sand and sandy loess.

21

April

Ackerland bei Warendorf, Nordrhein-Westfalen: In der Münsterländer Tieflandsbucht bestimmt Ackerbau das Landschaftsbild. Während der Nacht hat ein sanfter, aber kalter Luftstrom den Baum mit Reif überzogen.

Farmland near Warendorf, North Rhine-Westphalia. The landscape of the Münsterland basin is shaped by agriculture. In the night a gentle but cold wind has covered the tree with frost.

22

April

Inn bei Bad Füssing, Bayern: Neun Zehntel seines Weges hat der 517 Kilometer lange Inn bei Bad Füssing bereits hinter sich, bevor er dann in Passau in die Donau mündet. Links des Inselstreifens ist der Fluss zu sehen, rechts ein Altwasser.

The River Inn near Bad Füssing, Bavaria. At Bad Füssing, the Inn has covered nine tenths of its 517 kilometres, before it flows into the Danube in Passau. The river is to the left of the island; on the right is a backwater.

23

April

Forggensee, Bayern: Durch einen 41 Meter hohen Erddamm sperrte man in den 1950er Jahren bei Roß-haupten im Allgäu eine Lech-Schlucht ab. Der Ort Forggen versank, und ein zwölf Kilometer langer See entstand.

Forggensee, Bavaria. A 41 m high earth-fill dam was constructed in the 1950s near Rosshaupten in the Allgäu to block off a gorge on the river Lech. The town Forggen was submerged and a twelve kilometre long lake was created.

24

April

Talsperre Spremberg, Brandenburg: Seit 1965 staut man die Spree zwischen Spremberg und Cottbus. Die Talsperre schützt den Spreewald vor Hochwassern und stellt die Versorgung der nahe liegenden Braunkohlekraftwerke mit Kühlwasser sicher.

Spremberg reservoir, Brandenburg. Since 1965, the River Spree has been dammed between Spremberg and Cottbus. The reservoir protects the Spree Forest from flooding and secures the supply of water for cooling to neighbouring brown coal power stations.

25

April

Steinbruch bei Haldensleben, Sachsen-Anhalt: Der Flechtinger Höhenzug ist vulkanischen Ursprungs. Seit über hundert Jahren werden hier Vulkanite zum Straßen- und Gleisbau gebrochen. Der eisenhaltige Gesteinsstaub färbt sich in den Pfützen rot.

Quarry near Haldensleben, Saxony-Anhalt. The Flechtinger Höhenzug is a ridge of volcanic origin. For over one hundred years, vulcanite has been quarried for road and rail construction. The iron-rich rock dust turns red in the puddles.

26

April

Leipzig, Sachsen: Das Völkerschlachtdenkmal wurde 1913 nach 15-jähriger Bauzeit fertiggestellt. Der 91 Meter hohe Komplex erinnert an die größte Schlacht des 19. Jhs., die Völkerschlacht bei Leipzig, die 1813 vor den südlichen Toren der Stadt tobte.

Leipzig, Saxony. The Monument of the Battle of the Nations was completed in 1913 after 15 years of construction. The 91 m tall complex commemorates the biggest battle of the 19th century, the Battle of the Nations near Leipzig, which raged in 1813 beyond the southern gateway to the city.

27

April

Wasserschloss Irmelshausen, Bayern: Der fünfeckige Komplex entstand durch zahlreiche Umbauten. Eingang und Nordwestflügel des spätgotischen Fachwerkbaus stammen aus dem 15. Jh., drei weitere Flügel im Renaissancestil aus dem 16. Jh.

Wasserschloss Irmelshausen, Bavaria. The pentagonal palace evolved in the course of numerous renovations. The entrance area and northwest wing of the late gothic half-timbered building date back to the 15th century. Three further wings in renaissance style stem from the 16th century.

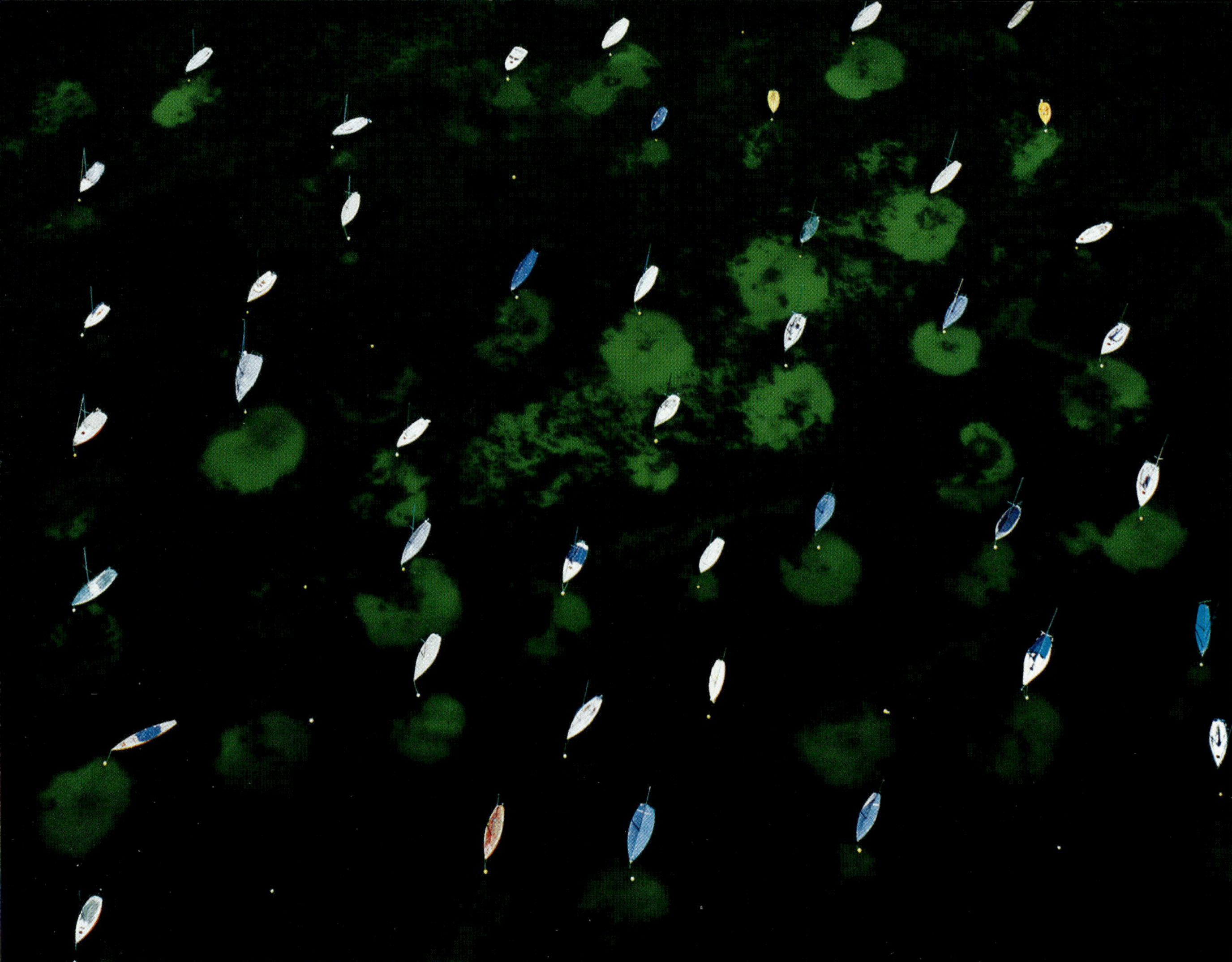

28

April

Segelboote auf dem Chiemsee, Bayern: Der achtzig Quadratkilometer große Chiemsee ist eines der beliebtesten Segelreviere Deutschlands. Rund um das »Bayerische Meer« verteilen sich offene Liegeplätze, Jachthäfen und ein Dutzend Segelschulen.

Sailing boats on Chiemsee, Bavaria. At eighty square kilometres in size, the Chiemsee is one of the most popular sailing locations in Germany. All around the »Bavarian Sea« there are moorings, marinas and a dozen sailing schools.

29

April

Passau, Bayern: Die Farben der Flüsse Inn und Ilz, die hier in die Donau münden, verraten schon etwas über ihre Herkunft: Der Inn bringt gelösten, hellen Steinstaub aus den Alpen mit; die Ilz führt moordunkles Wasser aus dem Bayerischen Wald zu.

Passau, Bavaria. The colours of the Rivers Inn and Ilz – which flow into the Danube here – reveal a bit about their sources. The Inn carries loose, light-coloured rock dust from the Alps, while the Ilz transports dark moorland water from the Bavarian Forest.

30

April

Mainschleife, Bayern:
Bei Volkach beschreibt der Main zwei markante Schleifen, die der Region ihren Namen gaben. Charakteristisch für Franken sind die dichte Besiedelung des Maintals, streifig zerstückelte Äcker, Weinberge und Spargelfelder.

Mainschleife, Bavaria. Near Volkach, the river Main makes two distinctive loops, giving the region its name (it means literally »loop in the Main«). The densely-populated Main valley, fragmented field systems, vineyards and asparagus fields are characteristic of Franconia.

1

Mai

Würzburg, Bayern: Alljährlich im Juli feiern die Würzburger das Kiliani-Volksfest. Gleichzeitig findet eine kirchliche Prozession statt, bei der die Gläubigen die Reliquien der Stadtheiligen Kilian, Kolonat und Totnan in den Kiliansdom tragen.

Würzburg, Bavaria. Every year in July, the people of Würzburg celebrate the Kiliani fair. At the same time a church procession takes place, with believers carrying relics of the city's patron saints Kilian, Kolonat and Totnan into the Kilian Cathedral.

2

Mai

Rapsfelder bei Aulendorf, Baden-Württemberg: Zur Gewinnung von Speiseöl musste man früher aufwändige Filter- und Extraktionsverfahren einsetzen, um die ungenießbare Erucasäure zu eliminieren. Bei modernen Rapssorten ist sie weggezüchtet.

Oilseed rape fields near Aulendorf, Baden-Württemberg. Complicated filter and extraction processes used to be necessary to remove the erucic acid when producing cooking oil. Modern rapeseed oil varieties, however, are cultivated without it.

3

May

Lübz bei Parchim, Mecklenburg-Vorpommern: Das Ackerland liegt auf einer Grundmoränenplatte mit zahlreichen Hügeln, Tälern und Seen. Die kleinen Wasserlöcher (»Sölle«), die überall in Mecklenburg-Vorpommern zu finden sind, sind Relikte der Eiszeit.

Lübz near Parchim, Mecklenburg-Western Pomerania. The farmland lies on a moraine ledge with numerous hills, valleys and lakes. The small water holes, called »Sölle« or kettle holes, which are to be found throughout Mecklenburg Western Pomerania, date back to the ice age.

4

Mai

Poel, Mecklenburg-Vorpommern: Die ersten Siedler der Ostseeinsel in der Wismarbucht rodeten im 13. Jahrhundert den reichen Baumbestand, um Ackerland zu gewinnen. Das Soll, eine Vertiefung in der Ackerfläche (unten), entstand während der Eiszeit.

Poel, Mecklenburg-Western Pomerania. The first settlers on the island in Wismar Bay in the Baltic Sea razed the sizeable tree population to the ground in the 13th century to make room for farmland. The kettle hole, a depression in the field (at the bottom), was formed in the ice age.

5

May

Wismar, Mecklenburg-Vorpommern: 2002 wurde die mittelalterliche Hansestadt in die UNESCO-Liste des Weltkulturerbes aufgenommen. 350 Baudenkmäler gibt es in der gut erhaltenen Stadt, darunter den 700 Jahre alten Turm der 1945 zerstörten Marienkirche.

Wismar, Mecklenburg-Western Pomerania. In 2002, this medieval Hanseatic City was added to the list of UNESCO World Heritage Sites. There are 350 historical buildings in the well-preserved town, including the 700 year old tower of the Marienkirche church, which was destroyed in 1945.

6

Mai

Ostholstein, Schleswig-Holstein: Auf einem Feld blüht Winterraps, eine Blattfrucht, die wegen ihrer ölhaltigen Samenkörner angebaut wird. Ein Hektar Raps liefert 1200 Liter Öl, das als Speiseöl oder zur Herstellung von Biodiesel verwendet wird.

Ostholstein, Schleswig-Holstein. Winter oilseed rape is blooming in a field. This non-cereal crop is cultivated for its oleiferous seeds. One hectare of oilseed rape generates 1200 litres of oil, which is used as cooking oil, or for the production of biodiesel.

7

May

Heiligenhafen, Schleswig-Holstein: Durch Wind und Strömung hat sich eine lange Nehrung gebildet, die von Westen nach Osten wandert. Der links zu sehende Teil ist inzwischen ein abgeschlossener Binnensee, im offenen Bereich rechts liegt der Hafen.

Heiligenhafen, Schleswig-Holstein. A long spit, which is drifting from west to east, has been formed by wind and currents. The part on the left is now an enclosed lake, and the harbour lies in the open area on the right.

8

Mai

Nord-Ostsee-Kanal, Schleswig-Holstein: Die meistbefahrene künstliche Wasserstraße der Welt führt von Brunsbüttel an der Elbe 95 km weit bis Holtenau an der Kieler Förde und verbindet somit Nord- und Ostsee. Sie ist bis 90 m breit und 11 m tief.

Kiel Canal, Schleswig-Holstein. The most-travelled man-made waterway in the world leads 95 km from Brunsbüttel on the Elbe river to Holtenau on the Firth of Kiel and connects the North Sea to the Baltic. It is 90 m wide and 11 m deep.

9

May

Petersdorf auf Fehmarn, Schleswig-Holstein: Die Kirche St. Johannis stammt aus dem 13. Jh. Ihren 64 Meter hohen Kirchturm nutzten die Seeleute schon im 16. Jh. als Tagesmarke, weil er aus bis zu zwanzig Seemeilen Entfernung zu erkennen ist.

Petersdorf on Fehmarn, Schleswig-Holstein. The St. Johannis church dates back to the 13th century. As far back as the 16th century, its 64 m high steeple was used by sailors as a landmark because it is recognisable from up to 20 nautical miles away.

10

Mai

Plön, Schleswig-Holstein: Bürgerhäuser, Adelshöfe, ein klassizistisches Rathaus, ein Schloss aus dem 17. Jh. und fünf Kirchen (im Bild: die Nikolaikirche) verleihen der Stadt am größten See des Naturparks Holsteinische Schweiz besonderen Charme.

Plön, Schleswig-Holstein. Houses, country estates, a neoclassical town hall, a palace dating back to the 17th century and five churches (the Nikolaikirche is shown in the picture) give a quite particular charm to the town on the biggest lake of the Holsteinische Schweiz Nature Park.

11

May

Baltrum, Niedersachsen: Wie alle sieben Ostfriesischen Inseln wandert auch die kleinste von ihnen, bedingt durch Meeresströmung und Wind, nach Osten. Die Häuser der rund 500 Bewohner von West- und Ostdorf sind in die Dünen hineingebaut.

Baltrum, Lower Saxony. The seven East Friesian islands, of which Baltrum is the smallest, are drifting eastwards due to ocean currents and wind. The houses of the 500 or so residents of Westdorf and Ostdorf are built into the dunes.

12

Mai

Lübbenau, Brandenburg: Die Aufnahme, kurz nach der Wiedervereinigung entstanden, zeigt die zu DDR-Zeiten unzulänglich gepflegten Agrarflächen. Optisch reizvoll, dem Ertrag jedoch abträglich ist das mit Klatschmohn durchsetzte Getreidefeld.

Lübbenau, Brandenburg. This photo, taken shortly after German reunification, shows the inadequate cultivation of agricultural land within the GDR. The corn poppies, which riddle this grain field, are beautiful to look at but detrimental to the harvest.

13

May

Lauchhammer, Brandenburg: Nur kurz diente die ehemalige Braunkohlegrube ab 1933 als Strandbad, dann drang schmutziges Grubenwasser ein. Schließlich nutzte man sie als Absetzbecken zur Aufbereitung des Wassers, mit dem die Kohle abgewaschen wird.

Lauchhammer, Brandenburg. The former brown coal mine only served as a lido for a short time from 1933 before dirty mine water intruded. Eventually it was used as a settling pond for treating the water used to wash the coals.

14

Mai

Neuenkirchen, Niedersachsen: Von Finkenwerder bis Stade erstreckt sich das Alte Land, das größte Obstanbaugebiet Nordeuropas. Auf dem sandig-tonigen Boden der linken Elbmarsch wachsen über drei Millionen Apfel-, Birn-, Pflaumen- und Kirschbäume.

Neuenkirchen, Lower Saxony. The Alte Land is the largest fruit-growing area in northern Europe. It stretches from Finkenwerder to Stade. Over three million apple, pear, plum and cherry trees grow in the sandy-clayey soil of the fens on the left bank of the Elbe.

15

May

Stemmen, Niedersachsen: Nicht Außerirdische sind verantwortlich für diese Spuren im Feld, sondern der Land-Art-Künstler Klaus Meyer-Warneboldt. 1992 pflügte er die Fisch-Vogel-Figur ins Brachland des Rittergutes Rössing bei Stemmen nahe Hannover.

Stemmen, Lower Saxony. The tracks in this field were not made by aliens, but by the Land Art artist Klaus Meyer-Warneboldt. In 1992 he ploughed the fish and bird figure into unused land belonging to Rössing Manor at Stemmen near Hanover.

16

Mai

Neubrandenburg, Mecklenburg-Vorpommern: Nach der Zerstörung 1945 folgte der Wiederaufbau den bereits 1248 angelegten rechtwinkligen Straßenzügen. Erhalten geblieben ist die alte Wall- und Wehranlage, die sich wie ein Ring um die Stadt schließt.

Neubrandenburg, Mecklenburg-Western Pomerania. After its destruction in 1945, the town's reconstruction observed the perpendicular street pattern which had dated back to 1248. The old city ramparts and fortifications, which form a ring round the town, have been retained.

17

May

Schloss Hohenbocka, Brandenburg: Von dem Ende des 19. Jhs. erbauten Schloss führt die Weinbergstraße durch einen alten Park zum Aussichtsturm auf dem Prossenberg. Er bietet Ausblick auf das größte Waldgebiet im Cottbuser Raum, die »Bucksche Schweiz«.

Schloss Hohenbocka, Brandenburg. The Weinberg Road leads from the palace, which was built at the end of the 19th century, through an old park to the viewing platform on the Prossenberg. It provides a panorama over the largest forest area in the Cottbus region, known as the »Bucksche Switzerland«.

18

Mai

Limburg, Hessen: Seit 1250 steht der siebentürmige Limburger Dom auf einem Felssporn über der Lahn. Seit der Außenrenovierung von 1965 erstrahlt das spätromanische Gotteshaus wieder in den ursprünglichen Farben Weiß und Rot.

Limburg, Hessia. Since 1250, the seven-towered Limburg Cathedral has stood on a rocky outcrop above the river Lahn. In 1965, exterior renovations returned the late-Romanesque church to its original resplendent colours of red and white.

19

May

Kassel, Hessen: Der Ursprung der Stadt als fränkischer Königshof spiegelt sich in den Straßen- und Platznamen wider: Auf den kreisrunden Königsplatz laufen die Untere und die Obere Königsstraße zu.

Kassel, Hesse. The names of the town's streets and squares reflect that its origins were as a Frankish royal court. The Lower and Upper Königsstraße (King Street) lead to the Königsplatz (King's Square).

20

Mai

Radfahrer bei Harsewinkel, Nordrhein-Westfalen: In über siebzig Prozent aller deutschen Haushalte findet sich mindestens ein Fahrrad. Nicht nur als stauunempfindliches Fortbewegungsmittel, auch in der Freizeitgestaltung hat das Zweirad Konjunktur.

Cyclists near Harsewinkel, North Rhine-Westphalia. In over seventy percent of all German households, there is at least one bike. Cycling is not just a means of transport for outsmarting the traffic jams, but it is also booming as a leisure pursuit.

21

May

Freudenberg, Nordrhein-Westfalen: Der historische Stadtkern der ehemaligen Bergarbeiterstadt zwischen Rothaargebirge und Westerwald ist eines der wenigen erhaltenen Beispiele einer deutschen Stadt mit geplantem Grundriss und einheitlichem Fachwerk.

Freudenberg, North Rhine-Westphalia. The historical centre of the former mine-workers' town between the Rothaar mountains and the Wester Forest is one of the few remaining examples of a planned German town with uniform half-timbered houses.

22

Mai

Kloster St. Blasien, Baden-Württemberg: Nachdem 1768 ein Feuer die Vorgängerkirche vernichtet hatte, gab der Fürstabt eine Kombination aus Klosterkirche und Mausoleum in Auftrag. So entstand die erste klassizistische Rotunde in Deutschland.

St Blasien Monastery, Baden-Württemberg. After a fire had destroyed the previous church in 1768, the Prince-Abbott commissioned a combination of minster and mausoleum. This is how Germany's first neo-Classical rotunda came into being.

23

May

Augsburg, Bayern: Die Fuggerei in der Jakobervorstadt ist die älteste Sozialsiedlung Europas. 1521 legte der reiche Jakob Fugger in einem Stiftungsbrief fest, dass in den 53 Häusern schuldlos verarmte Augsburger eine Unterkunft finden sollten.

Augsburg, Bavaria. The »Fuggerei« in the Jakobervorstadt part of the town contains the oldest almshouses in Europe. In 1521, the wealthy Jakob Fugger stipulated in a letter of endowment that the 53 houses should provide accommodation for citizens of Augsburg who had become poor through no fault of their own.

24

Mai

Spessart, Bayern: Jahrhundertelang war das 500 Meter hohe Mittelgebirge als Jagdrevier für geistliche und weltliche Herrscher reserviert. Deshalb ist es bis heute dünn besiedelt. Im nördlichen Teil wachsen vor allem Nadelbäume, im Süden Laubbäume.

Spessart, Bavaria. For centuries, the 500 m high mountain range was reserved as a hunting ground for religious and secular rulers. That's why, even today, it's thinly populated. In the northern part mainly coniferous trees grow; in the southern part, deciduous trees.

25

May

Münchner Flughafen, Bayern: Münchens neuer Flughafen liegt knapp 30 km nordöstlich der Landeshauptstadt im Erdinger Moos. Seit seiner Inbetriebnahme 1992 hat er sich zum zweitgrößten Airport von Deutschland entwickelt.

Munich Airport, Bavaria. Munich's new airport, in the Erdinger Moos area, is just under 30 km northeast of the Bavarian capital. Since it was opened in 1992, it has grown into Germany's second-biggest airport.

26

Mai

Günzburg, Bayern: Im Jahr 2002 eröffnete das Legoland Deutschland seine Tore. Über fünfzig Millionen Legosteine wurden für Figuren und detailgenau nachgebaute berühmte Städte und Gebäude zusammengesetzt.

Günzburg, Bavaria. In 2002, Legoland Germany opened its doors. Over fifty million lego bricks were assembled as figures and detailed models of famous towns and buildings.

27

May

Olympiapark, München: Markenzeichen der 1972 entstandenen Anlage sind die insgesamt fast 75 000 Quadratmeter großen Zeltdächer aus Acrylglasplatten, die das Olympiastadion, die Olympiahalle und die Olympia-Schwimmhalle überspannen.

Olympic park, Munich. The hallmark of the 1972 complex is the pavilion roofs which span the Olympic Stadium, Olympic Hall and Olympic Swimming Pool. They total almost 75,000 square metres in size and are made of plexiglass plates.

28

Mai

Frankenwald bei Kronach, Bayern: Nadelbäume lassen ihren Blütenstaub nicht von Insekten, sondern vom Wind übertragen. Dafür produzieren sie riesige Mengen. Hier zieht ein Staubsturm aus Fichtenpollen über den Wald.

Frankenwald near Kronach, Bavaria. Coniferous trees rely on the wind rather than insects to transfer their pollen, and produce huge amounts for this. Here, a dust storm of spruce pollen moves over the forest.

29

May

Burghausen, Bayern: Liebhaber von Burghausen nennen die tausend Jahre alte Stadt auch »Salzburg von Ostbayern«. Auf dem schmalen Bergrücken im Hintergrund erstreckt sich die mit 1100 Meter Ausdehnung längste Burg Deutschlands.

Burghausen, Bavaria. Burghausen enthusiasts also refer to the thousand year old town as »East Bavarian Salzburg«. At 1100 m in length, Germany's longest castle stretches along the narrow ridge in the background.

30

Mai

Starnberger See, Bayern: Der ungezähmte Natursee verwandelte sich im 17. und 18. Jh. zum Vergnügungsgewässer, als der Münchner Hof den großen Vorbildern von Venedig und Versailles nacheiferte. Bereits um 1850 verkehrten Dampfschiffe auf dem See.

Starnberger See, Bavaria. This untamed natural lake was transformed in the 17th and 18th centuries to a leisure lake, when the Munich court sought to emulate the courts of Venice and Versailles. As far back as 1850, steam ships were operating on the lake.

31

May

Wieskirche, Bayern: Umgeben von Wäldern und Hochmooren steht im oberbayerischen Voralpengebiet die Wallfahrtskirche »Zum gegeißelten Heiland auf der Wies«, kurz Wieskirche genannt. Sie gilt als eine der reinsten Schöpfungen des deutschen Rokoko.

Wieskirche, Bavaria. Surrounded by forest and upland moor, the pilgrims' church »Of Our Chastised Saviour in the Meadow«, known as the Meadow Church«, is located in Upper Bavaria, in the foothills of the Alps. It is considered one of the purest works of the German rococo period.

1

Juni

Bodensee, Bayern: Sein Becken haben Gletscher während vier Eiszeiten innerhalb von einer Million Jahren ausgeschürft. Der Bodensee ist rund 76 Kilometer lang und bis zu 14 Kilometer breit. An den tiefsten Stellen misst er um die 250 Meter.

Lake Constance, Bavaria. Its basin was created by glaciers in the course of four ice ages within one million years. Lake Constance is around 76 kilometres long and up to 14 kilometres wide. Its maximum depth is around 250 m.

2

June

Kaub, Rheinland-Pfalz: Der rechtsrheinische Ort ist bekannt für seinen Weinbau und für die Rheinüberquerung des Feldmarschalls Blücher, der hier in der Neujahrsnacht 1813/14 eine Pontonbrücke bauen ließ, um mit seinen Soldaten Napoleon zu verfolgen.

Kaub, Rhineland-Palatinate. The town to the right of the Rhine is famed for its wine-growing and for Field Marshal Blücher's crossing over the Rhine. He had a pontoon bridge built on New Year's Eve 1813–14 as he and his soldiers pursued Napoleon.

3

Juni

Holsteinisches Wattenmeer vor Büsum, Schleswig-Holstein: Immer wieder haben Unwetter die Nordseeküste verändert. Die Meldorfer Bucht reichte früher tiefer ins Land hinein, doch angespülter Schlick hat sich nach und nach als Marschland abgelagert.

Holstein Wadden Sea at Büsum, Schleswig-Holstein. Time and again, storms have altered the North Sea coast. Meldorf Bight used to reach further inland, but gradually washed up mud has deposited itself there as marshland.

4

June

Fehmarn, Schleswig-Holstein: Drei Naturschutzgebiete nehmen etwa 6 Kilometer der 78 km langen Küstenlinie der Insel ein: Grüner Brink, Krummsteert-Sulsdorfer Wiek und das Wasservogelreservat Wallnau, in dem 80 verschiedene Vogelarten brüten.

Fehmarn, Schleswig-Holstein. Three nature reserves cover around 6 km of the island's 78 km coastline: Grüner Brink, Krummsteert-Sulsdorfer Wiek and the water bird reserve Wallnau, in which 80 different types of bird breed.

5

Juni

Kieler Förde, Schleswig-Holstein: Zur traditionellen Windjammerparade während der Kieler Woche versammeln sich Briggs, Barken und Vollschiffe aus vielen Nationen auf der Innenförde. Die Kieler Woche ist das weltweit größte Segelsportereignis.

Firth of Kiel, Schleswig-Holstein. International brigs, barks and full rigged ships gather on the upper firth for the traditional windjammer parade during the Kieler Woche. The Kieler Woche is the largest sailing event in the world.

6

June

Kieler Förde, Schleswig-Holstein: Die Kieler Woche entstand aus einer Regatta, an der 1882 20 Jachten teilnahmen. Heute starten bei den Wettbewerben in der Kieler Förde, einem 17 km ins Land reichenden Meeresarm, bis zu 1600 Jollen und Jachten.

Firth of Kiel, Schleswig-Holstein. The »Kieler Woche« (Kiel Week) evolved from a regatta in 1882, in which 20 yachts participated. Nowadays up to 1600 dinghies and yachts take part in the races in the Firth of Kiel, an estuary which stretches 17 km inland.

7

Juni

Rönnauer Mühle, Schleswig-Holstein: Einst stand hier ein Ensemble aus Wind- und Wassermühle, Bäckerei, Brauerei und Gasthaus. 1970 riss man alle Gebäude am Stadtrand von Travemünde ab. Nur die Windmühle von 1840 wurde verschont.

Rönnau Windmill, Schleswig-Holstein. There used to be a windmill, watermill, bakery, brewery and an inn here. In 1970 all the buildings on the outskirts of Travemünde were pulled down. Only the windmill dating back to 1840 was left standing.

8

June

Fehmarn, Schleswig-Holstein: Die fast waldfreie Insel ist eine der regenärmsten und sonnenreichsten Regionen Deutschlands. Gerste-, Gemüse- und Rapsanbau sind weit verbreitet. Das Flügger Leuchtfeuer ist einer von vier Leuchttürmen auf der Insel.

Fehmarn, Schleswig-Holstein. The almost forest-free island is one of the driest and sunniest regions in Germany. There is widespread cultivation of barley, vegetables and oil seed rape. The Flügg lighthouse is one of four lighthouses on the island.

9

Juni

Ratzeburg, Schleswig-Holstein: Die Inselstadt verdankt ihren Namen dem Polabenfürsten Ratibor, genannt Ratse. Von der mittelalterlichen Stadt blieben nach einem Überfall der Dänen 1693 lediglich der Dom, die Petri-Kirche und fünf Häuser erhalten.

Ratzeburg, Schleswig-Holstein. The town on the island takes its name from the Polabian Prince Ratibor, nicknamed Ratse. Following a raid by the Danes in 1693, only the cathedral, the Petri Church and five houses were left standing in the medieval town.

10

June

Schloss Glücksburg, Schleswig-Holstein: Der vom Schlossteich umgebene Bau zählt zu den bedeutendsten Schlössern Nordeuropas. Er wurde zwischen 1582 und 1622 von Herzog Johann d. J. zu Schleswig-Holstein-Sonderburg errichtet.

Glücksburg Palace, Schleswig-Holstein. The building, which is surrounded by the palace lake, is one of the most important palaces in northern Europe. It was built between 1582 and 1622 by Duke Johann d. J. zu Schleswig-Holstein-Sonderburg.

11

Juni

Eibsee, Bayern: Der See am Fuß des Waxensteins verdankt seine Existenz dem größten Bergsturz der Bayerischen Alpen. Geröllmassen stürzten von der 2962 Meter hoch gelegenen Zugspitze herab und formten sein Becken auf 973 Meter Höhe.

Eibsee, Bavaria. The lake at the foot of the Waxenstein owes its existence to the largest rockslide in the Bavarian Alps. Masses of rubble plummeted down from the 2962 m high Zugspitze and formed its basin at a height of 973 m.

12

June

Walchensee, Bayern: Mit seinen 16,4 Quadratkilometern ist der Walchensee (802 m ü.d.M.) der größte und mit 192 Metern der tiefste deutsche Gebirgssee. Seine Ufer sind so gut wie unverbaut, wodurch der See rundum begehbar ist.

Walchensee, Bavaria. At 16.4 square kilometres, the Walchensee (802 m above sea level) is the largest German mountain lake. At 192 m deep, it's also the deepest. Its banks are almost completely undeveloped, making it possible to walk right round the lake.

13

Juni

Rheinfelden, Baden-Württemberg: Zwischen dem Hotzenwald als Südausläufer des Schwarzwaldes und den Aargauer Bergen der Schweiz schlängelt sich der Hochrhein an Bad Säckingen vorbei nach Rheinfelden.

Rheinfelden, Baden-Württemberg. Between the Hotze Forest, an offshoot to the south of the Black Forest, and the Aargau mountains of Switzerland, the High-Rhine snakes past Bad Säckingen to Rheinfelden.

14

June

Raststätte Illertal-Ost, Baden-Württemberg: Die Autobahnraststätte an der A 7 zwischen Memmingen und Ulm ist ein Gesamtkunstwerk. Sie wurde Mitte der 1990er Jahre von dem österreichischen Architekten und Künstler Herbert Maierhofer gestaltet.

The service station Illertal-Ost, Baden-Württemberg. The motorway service station on the A 7 between Memmingen and Ulm is, in its entirety, a work of art. It was designed in the mid-1990s by the Austrian architect and artist Herbert Maierhofer.

15

Juni

Willibaldsburg in Eichstätt, Bayern: Eine Schleife der Altmühl bildete den Jurafelssporn, auf dem die 1353 errichtete Burg liegt. Bis zum 18. Jh. residierten dort die Bischöfe von Eichstätt. Heute sind mehrere Museen darin untergebracht.

Willibaldsburg in Eichstätt, Bavaria. A loop in the Altmühl river formed the Jurassic spur of rock, upon which the castle dating back to 1353 stands. Until the 18th century, the bishops of Eichstätt lived there. Nowadays it is home to several museums.

16

June

Würzburg, Bayern: Napoleon nannte die Würzburger Residenz »Europas größten Pfarrhof«. Auftraggeber war 1720 Fürstbischof Johann Philipp Franz von Schönborn, der den Schlössern in Versailles und Schönbrunn etwas Ebenbürtiges zur Seite stellen wollte.

Würzburg, Bavaria. Napoleon called the Würzburg Residenz »Europe's biggest rectory«. It was commissioned in 1720 by Prince-Bishop Johann Philipp Franz von Schönborn, who wanted to create something equal in stature to the palaces of Versailles and Schönbrunn.

17

Juni

Bei Gorleben, Niedersachsen: Im Landkreis Lüchow-Dannenberg liegt das Erkundungsbergwerk Gorleben. Dort befindet sich ein drei Kilometer tiefer Salzstock, der von 1979 bis 2000 auf seine Eignung als Endlager für radioaktive Abfälle untersucht wurde.

Near Gorleben, Lower Saxony. The Gorleben pilot mine is in the district of Lüchow-Dannenberg. A salt deposit, three kilometres deep, was tested there from 1979 to 2000 for its suitability as a final storage for radioactive waste.

18

June

Lausitzring, Brandenburg: Wo bis in die 1980er Jahre Braunkohle im Tagebau gefördert wurde, fahren seit dem Jahr 2000 Autos und Motorräder um die Wette. Der Euro-Speedway Lausitz ist Europas modernste und größte Rennstrecke.

Lausitzring, Brandenburg. Until the 1980s, brown coal was open-cast mined here. ince 2000, it has been a racing track for cars and motorbikes. The Euro-Speedway Lausitz is Europe's most modern and largest racing track.

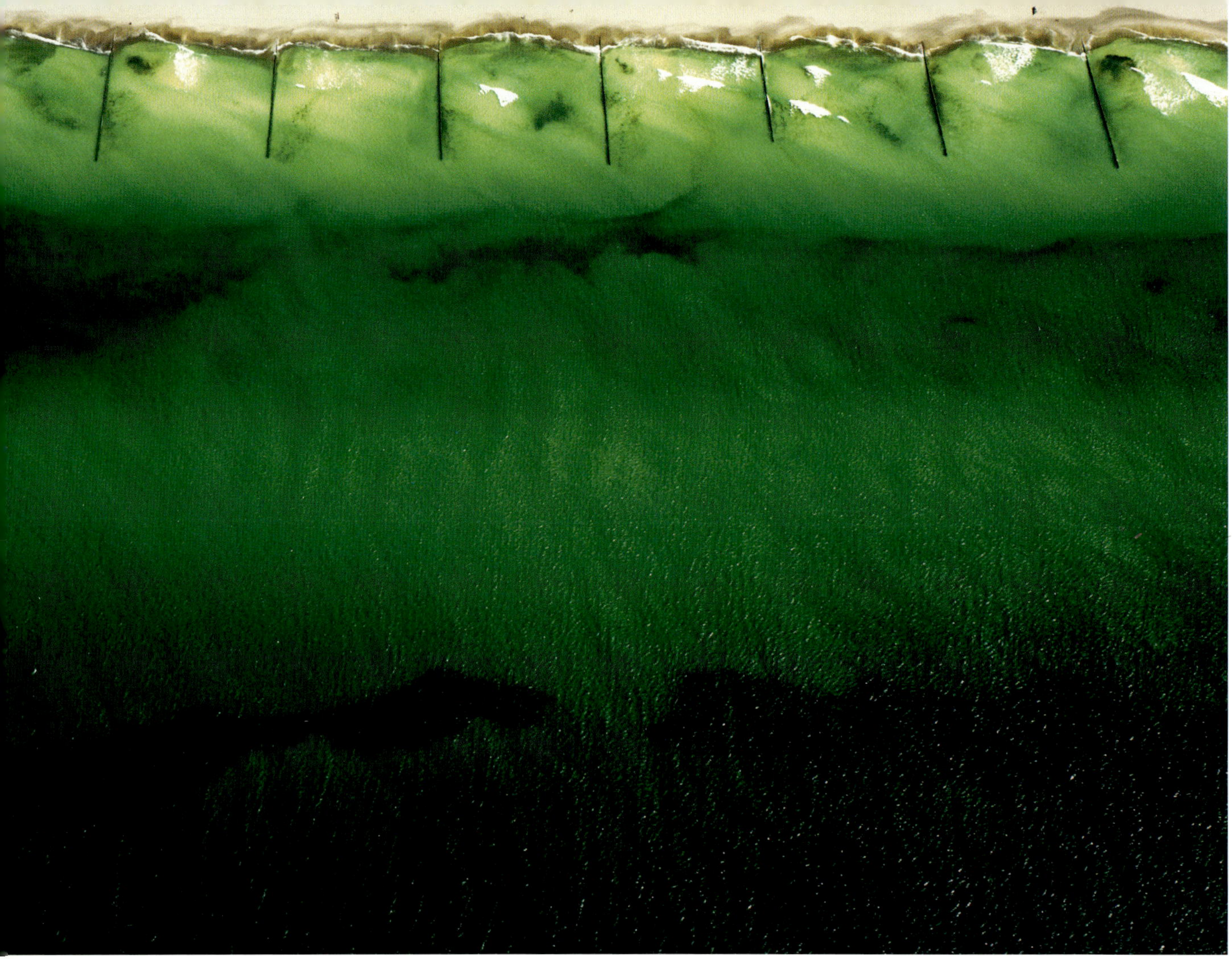

19

Juni

Nehrung Fischland, Mecklenburg-Vorpommern: Am Strand von Dierhagen versucht man, den Sand mit künstlichen Dämmen (Buhnen) festzuhalten. Die parallel zum Ufer verlaufende Strömung nimmt dennoch Material mit und lagert es weiter östlich wieder ab.

Fischland Spit, Mecklenburg-Western Pomerania. Efforts are being made to preserve the sand on the beach of Dierhagen by means of man-made causeways or dykes. The current which runs parallel to the shore however, carries sand away and deposits it further east.

20

June

Poel, Mecklenburg-Vorpommern: Die mit 37 qkm größte Insel Mecklenburgs ist ein staatlich anerkannter Erholungsort. Er zeichnet sich durch eine besonders gesunde Luft aus, die vor allem Asthmatikern und Allergikern Linderung verschaffen soll.

Poel, Mecklenburg-Western Pomerania. At 37 square metres, the largest island in Mecklenburg is an officially-recognised spa resort. The air is especially beneficial there, providing relief for asthmatics and people with allergies in particular.

21

Juni

Volkswagen-Werk in Wolfsburg, Niedersachsen: Unweit der Stelle, wo man einst vom Wasserschloss Wolfsburg aus den Übergang über die Aller kontrollierte, wurde 1938 das Volkswagen-Werk gegründet. Mit ihm entstand aus zwei Dörfern die Stadt Wolfsburg.

Volkswagen plant in Wolfsburg, Lower Saxony. Not far from the spot where the crossing over the river Aller used to be controlled from the moated castle of Wolfsburg, the Volkswagen plant was founded in 1938. The town Wolfsburg was created from two villages at the same time.

22

June

Bremerhaven, Bremen: Das Deutsche Schifffahrtsmuseum, eines der bedeutendsten weltweit, befindet sich dort, wo 1830 der ursprüngliche Bremer Hafen eröffnet wurde. Besonders sehenswert ist eine Hansekogge von 1380, die in der Weser gefunden wurde.

Bremerhaven, Bremen. The German Maritime Museum, one of the most important worldwide, is located where the original »Bremer Hafen« or Port of Bremen was opened in 1830. It is well worth seeing the Hanseatic Cog, a trading ship dating back to 1380, which was found in the river Weser.

23

Juni

Fürwiggetalsperre, Nordrhein-Westfalen: Die Talsperre sammelt Wasser, das am Kamm des Ebbegebirges zwischen Rothenstein und Kahlem Kopf abregnet. Der Bach Verse leitet das Wasser in die wenige Kilometer unterhalb gelegene Versetalsperre weiter.

Fürwiggetalsperre Reservoir, North Rhine-Westphalia. The dam collects rain water that flows from the ridge of the Ebbe mountains between Rothenstein and the Kahler Kopf. The Verse stream leads the water into the Versetal reservoir, which is situated a few kilometres further down.

24

June

Holzwickede, Nordrhein-Westfalen: Die Kleinstadt mit 17600 Einwohnern liegt in der Ballungsrandzone des östlichen Ruhrgebiets zwischen Dortmund und Unna. Am Marktplatz stehen die evangelische Kirche von 1907 und das Rathaus von 1915.

Holzwickede, North Rhine-Westphalia. The small town, with a population of 17,600, sits on the edge of the urban conglomeration of the eastern Ruhr area between Dortmund and Unna. The protestant church from 1907 and the town hall from 1915 are on the market square.

25

Juni

Festung Königstein, Sachsen: Im Jahr 1241 wurde die Burg im Elbsandsteingebirge erstmals als Grenzbefestigung der böhmischen Könige urkundlich erwähnt. Aufgrund ihrer unüberwindbaren Mauern und des weiten Sichtfelds wurde die Festung nie erobert.

Königstein Fort, Saxony. The castle in the Elbsandstein Mountains was first documented as a border fortification of the Bohemian kings in the year 1241. The fort was never taken due to its impenetrable walls and the long-range visibility from it.

26

June

Dresden, Sachsen: Unter August dem Starken und dessen Sohn Friedrich August II. wurde Dresden zwischen 1694 und 1783 zu einer der schönsten barocken Residenzstädte. Zu dieser Zeit entstanden das Taschenbergpalais, die Hofkirche und der Zwinger.

Dresden, Saxony. Between 1694 and 1783, under August the Strong and his son, Frederick August II, Dresden became one of the most beautiful baroque seats of power. The Taschenbergpalais, the Hofkirche (Court Church) and the Zwinger gallery were built during this time.

27

Juni

Kalibergwerk bei Zielitz, Sachsen-Anhalt: Seit 1973 gewinnt die Kali & Salz Gruppe in diesem Bergwerk nördlich von Magdeburg Kalisalz. Es dient hauptsächlich der Produktion von Düngemitteln, die weltweit eingesetzt werden.

Potash mine near Zielitz, Saxony-Anhalt. Since 1973, the Kali & Salz Gruppe has recovered potash salt in this mine north of Magdeburg. It is used primarily in the production of fertilisers, which are utilised worldwide.

28

June

Felder bei Hadmersleben, Sachsen-Anhalt: Nördlich der Mittelgebirge lagert in einem 20 bis 80 Kilometer breiten Gürtel fruchtbarer Lössboden. Er bildet den Grenzsaum zum norddeutschen Tiefland. Bereits seit der Steinzeit wird hier Getreide angebaut.

Fields near Hadmersleben, Saxony-Anhalt. North of the low level mountains, fertile loess soil forms a 20 to 80 km wide belt. It forms the boundary to the north German lowlands. Crops have been grown here since the Stone Age.

29

Juni

Bamberg, Bayern: 1993 erklärte die UNESCO den Stadtkern der Kaiser- und Bischofsstadt mit ihren über 2000 denkmalgeschützten Gebäuden zum Weltkulturerbe. Bamberg ist geprägt von mittelalterlicher und barocker Architektur.

Bamberg, Bavaria. In 1993, UNESCO added the centre of this imperial and diocesan town, with over 2000 protected buildings, to the list of World Heritage Sites. Bamberg is characterised by medieval and baroque architecture.

30

June

Schloss Seehof bei Bamberg, Bayern: Nachdem sich Franken vom Dreißigjährigen Krieg erholt hatte, drängte es die Fürsten wieder aufs Land. Ab 1686 ließ sich der Bamberger Fürstbischof das Schloss zwischen Wäldern und Karpfenteichen anlegen.

Seehof Palace near Bamberg, Bavaria. After Franconia had recovered from the Thirty Years' War, the sovereigns were lured back to the countryside. Bamberg's Prince-Bishop had the palace built from 1686 between forests and carp ponds.

1

Juli

KZ-Gedenkstätte Dachau, Bayern: Im 1933 errichteten ersten Konzentrationslager der Nationalsozialisten wurden über 30 000 Menschen ermordet. Neben den historischen Überresten erinnern daran heute ein Museum, ein Mahnmal und mehrere Sühnekapellen.

Dachau Concentration Camp Memorial, Bavaria. Over 30,000 people were murdered in the first concentration camp built by the National Socialists in 1933. Nowadays, as well as the historical remains of the camp, a museum, a monument and several chapels of atonement commemorate the dead.

2

July

Rapsfeld bei Gunzenhausen, Bayern: Im Altmühltal wächst der Raps auf Opalinuston. Dieser Boden kann viel Wasser aufnehmen und neigt dann zum Rutschen. Daran scheiterte 793 der Versuch Karls des Großen, einen Kanal zwischen Main und Donau zu graben.

Oilseed rape field near Gunzenhausen, Bavaria. In the Altmühl valley, oilseed rape grows on opaline clay. This soil can absorb a lot of water, which makes it prone to landslides. This thwarted Charlemagne's attempt to dig a canal between the rivers Main and Danube in 793.

3

Juli

Schwäbische Alb, Baden-Württemberg: Das südwestdeutsche Mittelgebirge fällt nach Nordwesten hin steil ins Vorland ab. 300 Meter unter dem Nebel verbergen sich Städte wie Göppingen, Esslingen und Stuttgart samt ihren Einzugsgebieten.

Swabian Alb, Baden-Württemberg. This low mountain range in the south-west of Germany drops sharply to the foreland in the north-west. Towns such as Göppingen, Esslingen and Stuttgart, and their catchment areas, are hidden 300 m under the fog.

4

July

Kaiserstuhl, Baden-Württemberg: Das vulkanische Gebirge in der oberrheinischen Tiefebene ist ideal für den Weinbau. Seine geringe Höhe und die geschützte Lage im Lee der Vogesen bewirken ein fast mediterranes Klima mit langen, warmen Sommern.

Kaiserstuhl, Baden-Württemberg. The volcanic mountains in the lowlands of the Upper Rhine are ideal for winegrowing. The low altitudes and wind shade provided by the Vosges mountains create an almost Mediterranean climate with long, warm summers.

5

Juli

Mainau, Bodensee:
Zur Römerzeit war sie eine militärische Anlage mit Kastell, Schiffswerft und Flottenbasis. Heute ist die Blumeninsel wegen ihrer Park- und Gartenanlagen mit subtropischen und tropischen Pflanzen ein beliebtes Ausflugsziel.

Mainau, Lake Constance. In Roman times, this was a military complex with a fort, shipyard and naval base. Today the »flower island« is a popular destination due to its gardens and parklands with subtropical and tropical plants.

6

July

Burg Hohenzollern, Baden-Württemberg: Wie ein Dornröschenschloss thront die Burg auf einem Kegelberg vor den Höhen der Schwäbischen Alb. Sie wurde Mitte des 19. Jhs. auf den Überresten einer älteren Burg im neugotischen Stil erbaut.

Hohenzollern Castle, Baden-Württemberg. The castle towers like Sleeping Beauty's palace on a cone-shaped mountain in front of the hills of the Swabian Alb. It was built in the middle of the 19th century in neo-Gothic style on the foundations of an older castle.

7

Juli

Burg Landeck, Rheinland-Pfalz: Um 800 wurden im Pfälzer Wald das Kloster Klingenberg und eine Turmburg errichtet, deren Ruine heute »das Schlössel« genannt wird. Ab dem 12. Jh. wachte die Burg Landeck als neue Schutzburg über die Benediktinermönche.

Landeck Castle, Rhineland-Palatinate. Around the year 800 in the Palatinate Forest, the monastery Klingenberg and a towered castle were built, the ruins of which today are known as the »Schlössel«. From the 12th century, Landeck Castle was the new fortress guarding the Benedictine monks.

8

July

Laacher See, Rheinland-Pfalz: Obwohl oft fälschlich als »größtes Eifelmaar« bezeichnet, ist der Laacher See kein Maar, sondern eine Caldera – der Einbruchkrater eines ehemaligen Vulkans. Es ist die einzige wassergefüllte Caldera Deutschlands.

Laach Lake, Rhineland-Palatinate. Although it is often incorrectly described as the »largest maar in the Eifel«, Laach Lake is not a maar but a caldera, or an irruption crater of a former volcano. It is the only water-filled caldera in Germany.

9

Juli

Pumpspeicherwerk Hohenwarte II, Thüringen: Das 293 Meter herabfallende Wasser treibt im Turbinenhaus die Generatoren an. Nachts, wenn im Netz überschüssiger Strom vorhanden ist, pumpt man Wasser aus dem Ausgleichsbecken nach oben.

Pumping plant and reservoir Hohenwarte II, Thuringia. Water cascades down 293 metres, powering the generators in the turbine house. At nighttime, when surplus electricity is available in the grid, water is pumped back up from the equalising reservoir.

10

July

Wartburg, Thüringen: Der Sage nach wurde die Burg 1067 von Ludwig dem Springer gegründet. Ihr heutiges Aussehen verdankt sie dem Wiederaufbau Mitte des 19. Jhs. 1521 übersetzte hier Martin Luther das Neue Testament in die deutsche Sprache.

Wartburg, Thuringia. According to legend, the castle was founded by Ludwig the Jumper in 1067. Its appearance today dates back to its reconstruction mid-19th century. In 1521, Martin Luther translated the New Testament into German here.

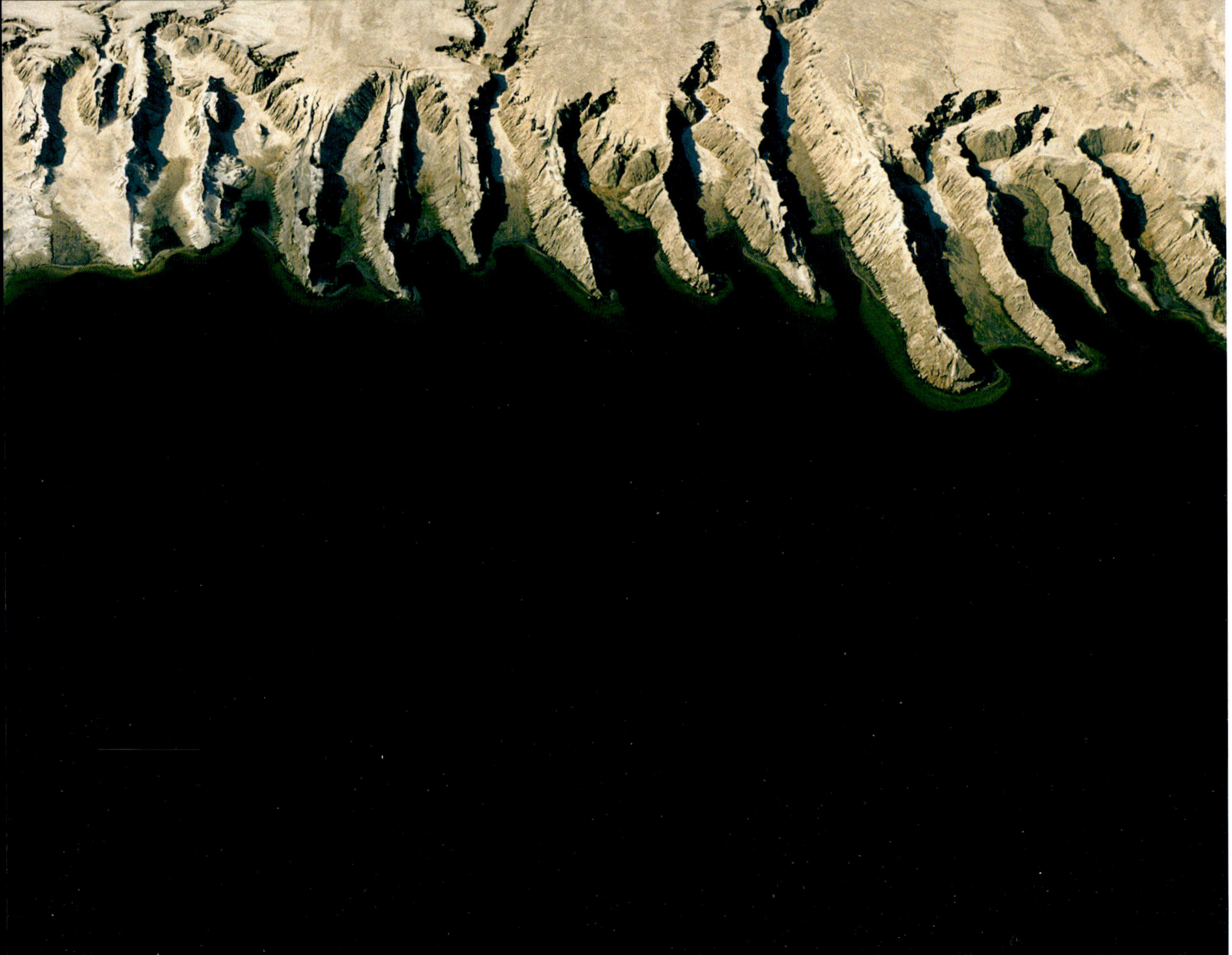

11

Juli

Bergbaufolgelandschaft bei Fürstlich Drehna, Brandenburg: Das ehemalige Braunkohletagebaugebiet liegt am östlichen Rand des Naturparks Niederlausitzer Landrücken. Grundwasser füllte die ausgebaggerten Mulden.

Post-mining landscape near Fürstlich Drehna, Brandenburg. The former brown coal open-cast mining area lies on the eastern edge of the Niederlausitzer Landrücken Nature Park. Groundwater fills the excavations.

12

July

Wasserschloss Groß Leuthen, Brandenburg: Seine Ursprünge hat das bei Lübben im Spreewald gelegene Wasserschloss im Mittelalter. 1913/14 wurde es um den Ostflügel, die vorgelagerte Terrasse und den Wohnturm erweitert.

Wasserschloss Groß Leuthen, Brandenburg. This moated castle near Lübben in the Spree Forest dates back to the middle ages. In 1913–14 it was extended to include an east wing, the front terrace and the residential tower.

13

Juli

Schloss Charlottenburg, Berlin: 1695 ließ Kurfürst Friedrich III. für seine Gemahlin Charlotte ein kleines Sommerschloss errichten. Nachdem er sich 1701 selbst zum König gekrönt hatte, erweiterte er das Schloss um die Seitenflügel und einen Ehrenhof.

Charlottenburg Palace, Berlin. In 1695, Elector Frederick III had a small summer palace built for his wife Charlotte. After he had crowned himself King in 1701, he extended the palace with side wings and a »cour d'honneur«.

14

July

Jagdschloss Grunewald, Berlin: Mitten im Grunewald ließ Joachim II., Kurfürst von Brandenburg, 1542 dieses Jagdschloss bauen. Heute birgt es ein Gemäldemuseum, ein Jagdzeugmagazin und eine Waldschule der Schutzgemeinschaft Deutscher Wald.

Jagdschloss Grunewald, Berlin. Joachim II, elector of Brandenburg, had this hunting lodge built in the middle of the Grunewald in 1542. Today it is home to a gallery, a hunting museum and a forest education centre run by the association for the protection of the German forest.

15

Juli

Großer Arber, Bayern: Der mit 1456 Metern höchste Berg des Bayerischen Waldes befindet sich im Besitz des Fürstenhauses Hohenzollern. Die Wiesenhänge, die von dem waldfreien Gipfel hinabführen, dienen im Winter als Skipisten.

Großer Arber, Bavaria. The highest mountain in the Bavarian Forest at 1456 m is owned by the royal house of Hohenzollern. The grassy slopes leading down from the treeless summit are used as ski runs in winter.

16

July

Hohenroth, Bayern: Das Straßendorf bei Bad Neustadt an der Saale war früher in Adelsbesitz. Ab dem 17. Jh. durfte die Gemeinde gegen eine jährliche Zinsleistung im Dorfteich Karpfen züchten. Im Sommer ist der Teich mit Schwimmfarn bedeckt.

Hohenroth, Bavaria. This one-street village near Bad Neustadt on the Saale used to be owned by the nobility. From the 17th century, the parish was allowed to breed carp in the village pond in return for an annual interest payment. In summer, the pond is covered by floating fern.

17

Juli

Maulbeeraue, Hessen: Nur eine kleine Brücke führt über einen Altwasserarm auf die 5 km lange Insel. Sie liegt auf der hessischen Seite des Rheins bei Biblis. Im 18. Jh. wurden hier Maulbeerbäume für die Seidenraupenzucht angepflanzt.

Maulbeeraue, Hesse. Only a small bridge leads over a stretch of backwater onto the 5 km long island. It lies on the Hessian side of the Rhine near Biblis. In the 18th century, mulberry trees were planted here for cultivating silkworms.

18

July

Papenburg, Niedersachsen: Die in Holland stark verbreitete Fehnkultur gibt es in Deutschland nur im Emsland. Bei der »Verfehnung« wird ein System von Kanälen geschaffen, um die Entwässerung eines Moores zu bewirken.

Papenburg, Lower Saxony. Fen cultivation, which is very common in Holland, is only seen in the Emsland area of Germany. This »de-fenning« involves constructing a network of canals to facilitate moor drainage.

19

Juli

Äcker bei Neetze, Niedersachsen: Ein Landwirt bewässert sein Feld. Das Ackerland liegt zwar unweit vom Urstromtal der Elbe, befindet sich aber auf der höher gelegenen Geestfläche, die durch trockene, sandige Böden gekennzeichnet ist.

Fields near Neetze, Lower Saxony. A farmer irrigates his field. The farmland is situated close to the watercourse of the Elbe, but lies on the higher geest, or sandy soil, areas which are characterised by dry sandy ground.

20

July

Northheim, Niedersachsen: Hinter dieser Botschaft steht die KWS Saat AG in Einbeck. Das Unternehmen ist seit 1856 im Bereich der Pflanzenzüchtung tätig. Umweltschutz wird großgeschrieben, auch Öko-Saatgut vertreibt das Unternehmen.

Northeim, Lower Saxony. The company KWS Saat AG in Einbeck is behind this message. It has operated in the plant breeding business since 1856. The company attaches utmost importance to environmental protection and also sells organic seeds.

21

Juli

Ochsenfurter Gau, Bayern: Die Agrarlandschaft in Unterfranken ist äußerst fruchtbar. Nach der Eiszeit wurde Gesteinsstaub dorthin verweht, der sich in mehrere Meter hohen Lössschichten ablagerte. Von Hand errichtete Strohböcke sind heute selten.

Ochsenfurter Gau, Bavaria. The farmland of Lower Franconia is extremely fertile. After the ice age, rock dust was blown there, settling in layers of loess soil several metres thick. These days handwoven corn dollies are rare.

22

July

Feld bei Roding, Bayern: Der Fluss Regen entsteht aus den Quellflüssen Weißer Regen und Schwarzer Regen, die sich im Bayerischen Wald vereinigen. Bei Roding weitet sich sein Tal und bietet Platz für die landwirtschaftliche Nutzung.

Field near Roding, Bavaria. The River Regen is formed by the headwaters Weißer Regen and Schwarzer Regen, which merge in the Bavarian Forest. Near Roding, the valley widens, giving scope for agricultural use.

23

Juli

Die Pulsnitz bei Ortrand, Brandenburg: Paddelbootfahrer nutzen die Natur auf eine äußerst sanfte Art. Allerdings ist beim An- und Ablegen Rücksicht auf Vögel geboten, die in der Röhrichtzone oder, wie der Regenpfeifer, auf den Kiesbänken brüten.

The Pulsnitz near Ortrand, Brandenburg. Canoeists use nature in a particularly gentle manner. However, when landing and casting off, they have to show consideration for the birdlife breeding in the reeds, or in the case of the plover, on the gravel banks.

24

July

Saarschleife bei Mettlach, Saarland: Wo sich Deutschland, Frankreich und Luxemburg ganz nahe sind, beschreibt die Saar auf ihrem Weg zur Mosel eine markante Schleife.

Loop in the River Saar near Mettlach, Saarland. Where Germany, France and Luxembourg meet, the Saar follows a distinctive loop on its way to the Moselle river.

25

Juli

Villa Borg, Saarland: In Perl/Stadtteil Borg wurde ab 1987 eine der größten römischen Villen im Saar-Mosel-Raum ausgegraben und nach wissenschaftlichen Erkenntnissen rekonstruiert. Im Herrenhaus befindet sich ein archäologisches Museum.

Villa Borg, Saarland. In the Borg area of Perl, excavation work began in 1987 of one of the largest roman villas in the Saar/Moselle area. Scientific know-how has enabled it to be reconstructed. An archaeolc gical museum is situated in the manor-house.

26

July

Losheim, Saarland: Seit 1982 betreibt der Museums-Eisenbahn-Club Losheim eine dampflokbetriebene Museumsbahn auf den Gleisanlagen der ehemaligen Merzig-Büschfelder-Eisenbahn (MBE). 1987 wurden Bahnstrecke und Gebäude unter Denkmalschutz gestellt.

Losheim, Saarland. Since 1982, the Museums-Eisenbahn-Club Losheim has run a steam-powered museum railway on the tracks of the former Merzig-Büschfelder-Eisenbahn (MBE). In 1987, the tracks and buildings were made listed buildings.

27

Juli

Blumenanbau bei Aschaffenburg, Bayern: Man könnte vermuten, diese Aufnahme sei in Holland entstanden. Aber auch am bayerischen Untermain werden Blumen in großem Stil angebaut. Das günstige Klima des Rhein-Main-Gebietes macht es möglich.

Flower plantation near Aschaffenburg, Bavaria. You would almost guess this photo was taken in Holland, yet flower farming also takes place on a large scale on the lower Main region of Bavaria, thanks to the favourable climate of the Rhine-Main area.

28

July

Günzburg, Bayern: 52 Freizeitparks locken in Deutschland Jahr für Jahr mehr als zwanzig Millionen Besucher an. Das Legoland setzt vor allem auf Autofahrer. Zu der Erlebniswelt aus bunten Plastiksteinen gehört ein Parkplatz für 4000 Personenwagen.

Günzburg, Bavaria. 52 leisure parks in Germany attract more than twenty million visitors each year. Legoland pins its hopes largely on visitors by car. The wonderful world of colourful plastic bricks has parking spaces for 4000 cars.

29

Juli

Querfurter Börde, Sachsen-Anhalt: Aufgrund einer mehrere Meter dicken Lössschicht ist das Ackerland äußerst fruchtbar. Eingeschränkt wird die Nutzung allerdings durch artesisch aufsteigendes Grundwasser, wodurch stellenweise Staunässe entsteht.

Querfurter Börde, Saxony-Anhalt. The farmland here is particularly fertile, due to a layer of loess soil which is several metres thick. Its utilisation is, however, restricted by artesian groundwater, which leaves the soil waterlogged in places.

30

July

Felder bei Annaberg, Sachsen: Die Nähe zur unberührten Natur des Naturparks Erzgebirge-Vogtland erfreut den Besitzer dieser Felder nur wenig: Um »Unkräuter« abzuhalten, spritzte er Unkrautvernichtungsmittel entlang der Ackerränder.

Fields near Annaberg, Saxony. The owner of these fields is not particularly impressed by his proximity to the unspoiled nature of the Nature Park Erzgebirge-Vogtland. To prevent »weeds«, he has sprayed weed killer along the edges of the field.

31

Juli

Chiemsee, Bayern: Von Gstadt und Prien aus fahren Schiffe im Linienverkehr zur Herreninsel mit dem Königsschloss Ludwigs II. und zur Fraueninsel mit dem Benediktinerinnenkloster Frauenwörth. Die dazwischen liegende kleine Krautinsel ist unbewohnt.

Chiemsee, Bavaria. Boats operate a regular service from Gstadt and Prien to the Herreninsel, with Louis II's royal palace, and the Fraueninsel, with its Benedictine convent Frauenwörth. The small Krautinsel, which lies between the two larger islands, is uninhabited.

1

August

Chiemsee, Bayern: Der Chiemsee ist eines der beliebtesten Segelreviere Deutschlands. Grundsätzlich ist diese Freizeitbeschäftigung umweltschonend. Eine Belastung des Wassers stellen allerdings die chemischen Antialgenmittel auf dem Bootsrumpf dar.

Chiemsee, Bavaria. The Chiemsee is one of the most popular sailing areas in Germany. This leisure pursuit is basically environmentally friendly, although the anti-algae chemicals on the hulk of the boats are a pollutant.

2

August

Pfälzer Wald, Rheinland-Pfalz: Das Bundsandsteinbergland mit Höhen bis 673 m wurde 1958 unter Landschaftsschutz gestellt. Im November 1992 wurde der »Naturpark Pfälzerwald« von der UNESCO als Biosphärenreservat anerkannt.

Palatinate Forest, Rhineland-Palatinate. The new red sandstone highlands, at up to 673 m in height, were made a conservation area in 1958. In November 1992, the Palatinate Forest Nature Park was declared a Biosphere Reserve by UNESCO.

3

August

Nürburgring, Rheinland-Pfalz: Seit seiner Einweihung 1927 hat sich der Nürburgring zu einer der bedeutendsten Rennstrecken der Welt entwickelt. Er besteht aus zwei Rundkursen: der Nordschleife und dem 4,5 Kilometer langen Grand-Prix-Kurs.

Nürburgring, Rhineland-Palatinate. Since its inauguration in 1927, the Nürburgring has become one of the most important racing tracks in the world. It is made up of two circuits, the North Loop and the 4.5 km Grand Prix track.

4

August

Brand, Brandenburg: Die Cargo-Lifter AG errichtete auf dem Gelände des ehemaligen russischen Luftwaffenstützpunkts Brand die größte freitragende Halle der Welt. Bis zu ihrem Konkurs im Jahr 2002 wurden hier Zeppeline gebaut.

Brand, Brandenburg. The company Cargo-Lifter AG constructed the biggest cantilevered hall in the world on the grounds of the former Russian air force base in Brand. Zeppelins were built here until the company went bankrupt in 2002.

5

August

Nationalpark Unteres Odertal, Brandenburg: Als Grenzfluss zu Polen blieb die Oder unreguliert und bildete auf über 60 km Länge eine artenreiche Auenlandschaft aus. Im 1995 eröffneten Nationalpark brüten viele seltene Vogelarten.

Lower Oder Valley National Park, Brandenburg. The Oder, as the river border to Poland, was largely left to nature. Over a stretch of more than 60 km, a floodplain with a huge variety of species developed. Many rare birds breed in the National Park which opened in 1995.

6

August

Elbe-Havel-Kanal, Brandenburg: Die Wasserstraße entstand durch den Ausbau des Plauer Kanals und des Ihlekanals. Bereits 1743–1745 ließ der Preußenkönig Friedrich II. den Plauer Kanal im Rahmen eines Trockenlegungsprojekts zur Landgewinnung anlegen.

Elbe-Havel Canal, Brandenburg. The waterway was created by the extension of the Plau and Ihle Canals. As far back as 1743–1745, King Frederick II of Prussia had the Plau Canal constructed as part of a drainage project for land reclamation.

7

August

Schlepzig, Brandenburg: Der 640-Einwohner-Ort im Herzen des Unterspreewaldes wurde am 8. August 1004 erstmals urkundlich erwähnt, als Heinrich II. ihn dem Kloster zu Nienburg schenkte. Die Fachwerkkirche stammt aus dem Jahr 1782.

Schlepzig, Brandenburg. This village – with a population of 640 – in the heart of the lower Spree Forest was first mentioned in records on the 8th August 1004, when Henry II gave it to the Nienburg monastery. The half-timbered church dates back to the year 1782.

8

August

Ackerland bei Alsfeld, Hessen: Im hessischen Hügelland nördlich des Vogelsbergs zwischen Alsfeld und Schlitz liegen weite Wiesenflächen. Üblicherweise werden hier drei Grasernten pro Jahr eingefahren und frisch oder als Heu ans Vieh verfüttert.

Farmland near Alsfeld, Hesse. Wide expanses of meadow are found in the rolling countryside of Hesse, north of the Vogelsberg mountains between Alsfeld and Schlitz. Typically, the grass here is harvested three times a year and fed to cattle either fresh or as hay.

9

August

Schafweide bei Schlüchtern, Hessen: Schafe erhalten Kulturlandschaften. Denn sie fressen außer Gras und Kräutern auch die jungen Sprosse von Bäumen und Büschen. So bewahren sie das typische Landschaftsbild der Rhön mit ihren freien Wiesenflächen.

Sheep-run near Schlüchtern, Hesse. Sheep preserve cultivated landscapes by grazing on the young shoots from trees and bushes, as well as on grass and weeds. This conserves the typical landscape of the Rhön area with its open meadowlands.

10

August

Insel Reichenau, Baden-Württemberg: Obst, Gemüse und Sonderkulturen brauchen neben dem richtigen Boden auch das passende Klima. Die Insel Reichenau im Bodensee bietet den Pflanzen und den Landwirten davon reichlich.

Reichenau island, Baden-Württemberg. Fruit, vegetables and arable crops require the right soil as well as a suitable climate. The island of Reichenau on Lake Constance provides plants and farmers with plenty of both.

11

August

Heidelberg, Baden-Württemberg: Seit 1386 ist Heidelberg Universitätsstadt. Der Universitätsplatz liegt rechts der langen Hauptstraße, die zum Marktplatz mit dem weißen Rathaus und der Heiliggeistkirche führt.

Heidelberg, Baden-Württemberg. Heidelberg has been a university town since 1386. The Universitätsplatz is to the right of the long Hauptstraße, which leads to the Marktplatz with its white town hall and the Heiliggeistkirche (Church of the Holy Spirit)

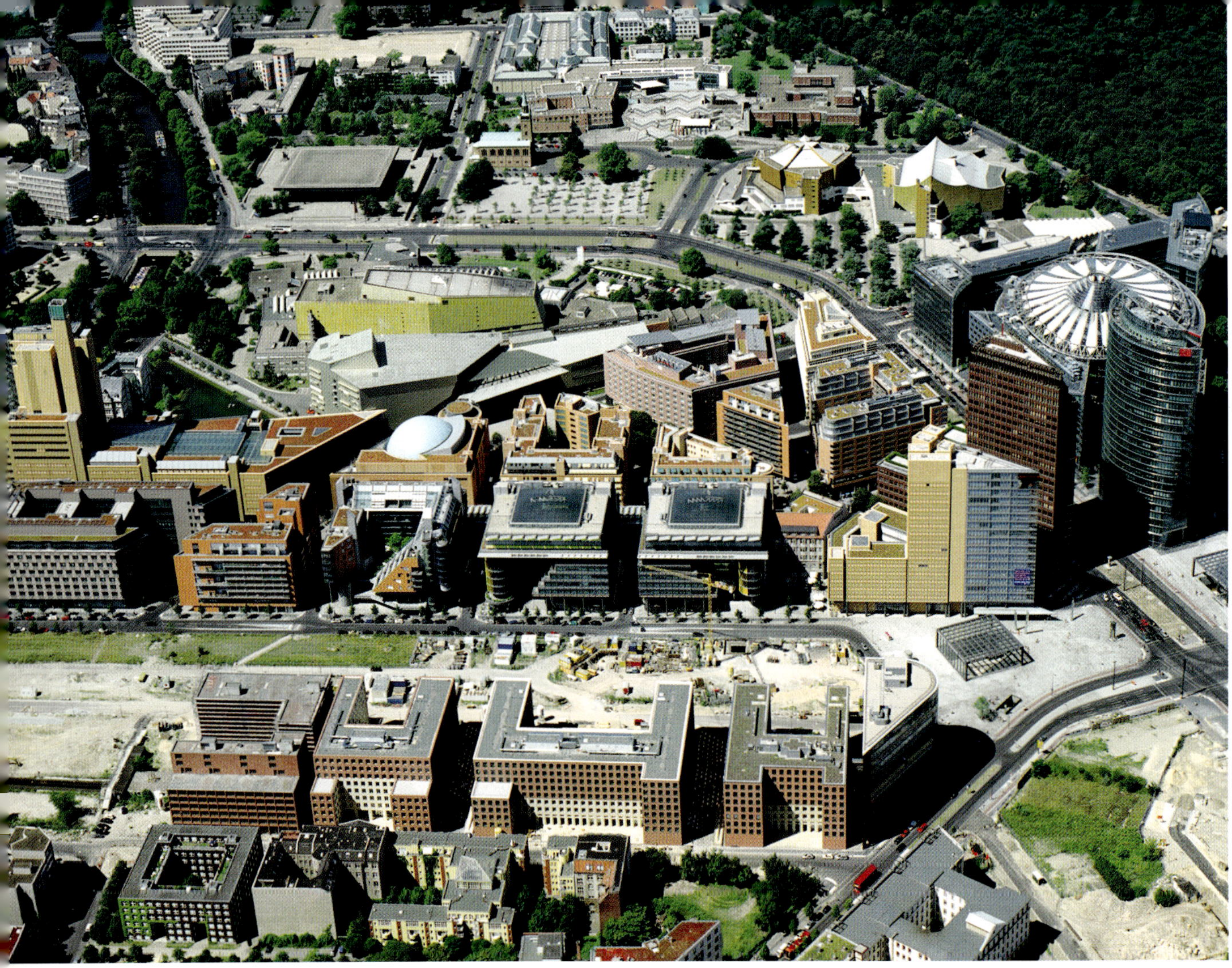

12

August

Berlin Mitte: Bis 1990 war der Potsdamer Platz ein von der Mauer durchschnittenes Niemandsland. Nach der Wiedervereinigung gestalteten namhafte Architekten moderne Bauten aus Stein, Stahl und Glas, wie Sony-Center mit seinem Zeltdach (rechts).

Berlin Mitte. Until 1990, Potsdamer Platz was a no-man's land, bisected by the Berlin Wall. After reunification, renowned architects designed modern buildings made of stone, steel and glass, such as the Sony-Center with its pavilion roof (on the right).

13

August

Baustelle Spreebogen, Berlin: Am 20. Juni 1991 beschloss der Deutsche Bundestag, die Regierung von Bonn nach Berlin zu verlegen. Als zentraler Standort der Neubauten wurde der Spreebogen in unmittelbarer Nachbarschaft des Reichstagsgebäudes bestimmt.

Building site on the Spreebogen, Berlin. On the 20th June 1991, the German parliament decided to move the government from Bonn to Berlin. The Spreebogen (or bend in the River Spree) was earmarked as the central location for the new buildings due to its proximity to the parliament building.

14

August

Schloss Sanssouci in Potsdam, Brandenburg: Einen Traum erfüllte sich der Preußenkönig Friedrich der Große mit dieser Schlossanlage. Als Staatsmann, Poet, Philosoph und Flötenspieler wollte er hier ein Leben ohne Sorge führen – sans souci.

Palace of Sanssouci, Potsdam, Brandenburg. This palace complex was a dream come true for the Prussian King Frederick the Great. This statesman, poet, philosopher and flautist wanted to live his life here without any worries – quite literally, sans souci.

15

August

Botanischer Garten, Berlin: Die Anlage im Berliner Stadtteil Dahlem wurde um 1900 von dem Botaniker Adolf Engler geschaffen. Mit über 22 000 Pflanzenarten ist sie einer der umfangreichsten und wissenschaftlich bedeutendsten botanischen Gärten der Erde.

Botanic Gardens, Berlin. The complex in the Dahlem area of Berlin was established by the botanist Adolf Engler around 1900. With over 22,000 species of plant, it is one of the most comprehensive and scientifically significant botanic gardens world wide.

16

August

Ingolstadt, Bayern: Die Ingolstädter Altstadt ist von einem mittelalterlichen Mauerring umgeben. Innerhalb davon stehen die Häuser in Giebelstellung zur Straße und geben so ein Zeugnis altbayerischen Städtebaus.

Ingolstadt, Bavaria. Ingolstadt's old town is surrounded by a medieval wall. Within this, the houses stand gable-end to the road, which is characteristic of old Bavarian town planning.

17

August

Wasserburg, Bayern: Am Inn-Übergang der Salzhandelsstraße von Reichenhall nach München ließ Hallgraf Engelbert im 12. Jh. eine »Burg am Wasser« errichten. Die nahe gelegene Fischersiedlung entwickelte sich in der Folge zur Stadt.

Wasserburg, Bavaria. Where the salt trade road from Reichenhall to Munich crosses the River Inn, Hallgraf Engelbert had a »castle on the water« built in the 12th century. The fisher-men's settlement nearby grew into a town as a result of this.

18

August

Kloster Weltenburg, Bayern: Bei Weltenburg hat sich die Donau fünf Kilometer durch den Fränkischen Jura geschnitten und das gewaltigste Durchbruchtal Deutschlands geschaffen. Wandermönche gründeten hier im 8. Jh. das älteste Kloster Bayerns.

Weltenburg Monastery, Bavaria. At Weltenburg, the Danube has cut a five kilometre ravine through the Franconian Jura, creating the biggest gorge in Germany. Missionary monks established the oldest monastery in Bavaria here in the 8th century.

19

August

Wallfahrtskirche Vierzehnheiligen, Bayern: Der Legende nach erschienen im Jahr 1445 in der Nähe des Klosters Langheim einem Schäfer die 14 Nothelfer. An dieser Stelle errichtete man eine kleine Kapelle und 300 Jahre später eine große Barockkirche.

Vierzehnheiligen Pilgrimage Church, Bavaria. According to legend, in the year 1445, fourteen helpers appeared to a shepherd in his hour of need near Langheim Monastery. A small chapel was erected here, followed 300 years later by a large baroque church.

20

August

Reußenköge, Schleswig-Holstein: Im Marschland von Nordfriesland ist ein Windpark errichtet worden, der inzwischen einen bedeutenden Beitrag zur Erzeugung umweltfreundlicher Energie erbringt. Denn Mangel an Wind besteht in Küstennähe nicht.

Reußenköge, Schleswig-Holstein. A wind farm has been built on the fens of North Friesia. Since then it has made an important contribution to the production of environmentally friendly energy, for there is no shortage of wind by the coast.

21

August

Eider, Schleswig-Holstein: Der Fluss entspringt südlich des Bothkamper Sees. Statt den kurzen Weg zur Ostsee zu wählen, windet er sich westwärts bis zur Nordsee, wo das 4,8 km breite Eidersperrwerk den Ort Tönning vor Sturmfluten schützt.

Eider, Schleswig-Holstein. The river rises south of the Bothkamper See. Instead of taking the shorter route to the Baltic Sea, it winds westwards to the North Sea where the 4.8 km wide Eider flood barriers protect the town of Tönning from storm tides.

22

August

Nehrung bei Damp, Schleswig-Holstein: Entlang der Eckernförder Bucht reiht sich ein Campingplatz an den anderen. Dieser Abschnitt der Ostsee ist durch einen 25 Kilometer langen, durchgehenden Sandstrand gekennzeichnet.

Spit near Damp, Schleswig-Holstein. There is one campsite after another along Eckernförder Bay. This section of the Baltic Sea is characterised by a 25 kilometre continuous stretch of beach.

23

August

Brunsbüttel, Schleswig-Holstein: Die Stadt an der Elbmündung ist vor allem als Schleusenhafen des Nord-Ostsee-Kanals bekannt, der Schiffen den Weg um Skagen erspart und die Strecke von der Nord- zur Ostsee um rund 460 Kilometer verkürzt.

Brunsbüttel, Schleswig-Holstein. The town on the estuary of the Elbe is well-known mainly as the gateway to the Kiel Canal, which saves ships sailing around Skagen and shortens the route from the North Sea to the Baltic by around 460 km.

24

August

Müritz-Nationalpark, Mecklenburg-Vorpommern: Zwischen Neustrelitz und dem Müritzsee erstreckt sich der 1990 gegründete Nationalpark. Für die innere Schutzzone gilt: Betreten verboten! In den äußeren Bereichen gibt es 500 Kilometer Wanderwege.

Müritz National Park, Mecklenburg-Western Pomerania. The National Park, which was established in 1990, stretches from Neustrelitz to the Müritz see. The inner area of the park is cordoned off to the public, but the outer areas feature 500 kilometres of footpaths.

25

August

Fischland, Mecklenburg-Vorpommern: Noch vor wenigen Jahrhunderten befand sich an der Stelle der Halbinsel Fischland–Darß–Zingst eine Kette aus unverbundenen Inseln. Durch Stürme und die Strömungen der Ostsee wuchsen sie jedoch zusammen.

Fischland, Mecklenburg-Western Pomerania. Just a few centuries ago, a chain of separate islands were situated where the Fischland-Darß-Zingst peninsula now lies. They grew together, however, due to storms and currents in the Baltic Sea.

26

August

Rostock, Mecklenburg-Vorpommern: Gegenüber dem Seehafen liegen am linken Ufer der Unterwarnow die Plattenbausiedlungen Groß Klein und dahinter Lichtenhagen. Entlang der Ostsee erstreckt sich der Sandstrand von Warnemünde.

Rostock, Mecklenburg-Western Pomerania. Opposite the seaport on the left bank of the Unterwarnow river lie the prefabricated high-rise estates Groß Klein and, behind it, Lichtenhagen. The sandy beach of Warnemünde stretches along the Baltic coast.

27

August

Seehafen von Rostock, Mecklenburg-Vorpommern: Der Hafen liegt am rechten Warnowufer einige Kilometer meerwärts von der Stadt entfernt. Auf über 9000 Meter Kailänge stehen 43 Schiffsliegeplätze zur Verfügung.

Seaport of Rostock, Mecklenburg-Western Pomerania. The port lies on the right bank of the Warnow river, a few kilometres seawards from the town. 43 berths for ships are available on over 9000 metres of quayside.

28

August

Autobahnkreuz Schönefeld, Brandenburg: Die helle Autobahn ist die von Dresden kommende A 13, die nach dem Schönefelder Kreuz als A 113 nach Berlin weiterführt. Sie kreuzt sich hier mit der A 10, die vom Ruhrgebiet nach Frankfurt an der Oder verläuft.

Motorway interchange Schönefeld, Brandenburg. The light-coloured motorway is the A 13 from Dresden, which continues to Berlin as the A 113 after the Schönefeld interchange. It intersects here with the A 10, which runs from the Ruhr area to Frankfurt (Oder).

29

August

Tiergarten, Berlin: Der größte Innenstadtpark Berlins wird von der Straße des 17. Juni durchschnitten. An dieser Straße steht das 1945 errichtete Sowjetische Ehrenmal, das an die im Kampf um Berlin gefallenen Sowjetsoldaten erinnert.

Tiergarten, Berlin. The largest city centre park in Berlin is intersected by the Straße des 17. Juni. The Soviet cenotaph, erected in 1945, is on this street and commemorates the Soviet soldiers killed in the battle for Berlin.

30

August

Wannsee, Berlin: Das Gewässer beim Stadtteil Wannsee, das als Berliner Ausflugsziel par excellence gilt, setzt sich aus mehreren verbundenen Seen zusammen: Kleiner und Großer Wannsee, Pohlesee, Stölpchensee und Griebnitzsee.

Wannsee, Berlin. The stretch of water in the Wannsee district is made up of several conjoined lakes: the Kleiner and Großer Wannsee, Pohlesee, Stölpchensee and Griebnitzsee. It is considered to be Berlin's leisure destination par excellence.

31

August

Pfaueninsel, Berlin; König Friedrich Wilhelm II. ließ seiner Mätresse Wilhelmine Encke 1794 bis 1796 auf der Pfaueninsel in der Havel ein Lustschloss errichten. Wilhelmine Encke soll den Bau im romantischen Ruinenstil selbst skizziert haben.

Pfaueninsel, Berlin. King Frederick William II had a summer residence built on the Pfaueninsel (Peacock Island) on the Havel river from 1794 to 1796 for his mistress Wilhelmine Encke. It is claimed Wilhelmine Encke sketched the design for the romantic ruined-style building herself.

1

September

Bei Iphofen, Bayern: Der Untergrund dieser fränkischen Landschaft besteht aus Gipskeuper, der für die Region eine große wirtschaftliche Bedeutung hat: Im Tage- und Untertagebau wird Gips gewonnen und vor Ort weiterverarbeitet.

Near Iphofen, Bavaria. The bedrock of this Franconian landscape is made up of gypseous Keuper, which is of great economic importance for the region. Gypsum is recovered using open-cast and deep mining and is processed locally.

2

September

Felder bei Grafenrheinfeld, Bayern: Das Ackerland südlich der fränkischen Industriestadt Schweinfurt war im Altertum mit Wald bedeckt. Heute ist nur noch ein Fünftel der Fläche mit Buchen, Eichen und Kiefern bestanden.

Fields near Grafenrheinfeld, Bavaria. The farmland to the south of the Franconian industrial town of Schweinfurt was covered with forest in ancient times. Today only a fifth of the area survives as forest, containing beech, oak and pine trees.

3

September

Kloster Banz, Bayern: Das Gebäude, das sich auf einem Ausläufer der Haßberge erhebt, fungierte in seiner über tausendjährigen Geschichte als Burg, Benediktinerkloster, Schloss der Wittelsbacher, wieder als Kloster und seit 1978 als Bildungszentrum.

Banz Monastery, Bavaria. The building, elevated on a foothill of the Haßberge, has – in its over one thousand year history – been used as a castle, a Benedictine monastery, a Wittelsbacher palace, a monastery once again and, since 1978, an education centre.

4

September

Schloss Augustusburg, Sachsen: Das einstige Jagd- und Lustschloss ließ Kurfürst August I. von 1568 bis 1572 auf dem Schellenberg errichten, einem weithin sichtbaren, 516 Meter hohen Quarz-Porphyr-Kegel über dem Tal der Zschopau.

Augustusburg Palace, Saxony. Elector August I had the former hunting lodge and summer residence built between 1568 and 1572 on the Schellenberg, a 516 metre high quartz and porphyry cone, visible from afar, above the Zschopau valley.

5

September

Neuendorfer Bülten, Mecklenburg-Vorpommern: Die Inselgruppe liegt von der Ostsee abgeschirmt im Saaler Bodden. Sie gehört zu dem 1990 gegründeten Nationalpark Vorpommersche Boddenlandschaft.

Neuendorfer Bülten, Mecklenburg-Western Pomerania. The group of islands lies in the Saaler Bodden protected from the Baltic Sea. They are part of the West-Pomeranian Boddenlandschaft National Park, which was established in 1990.

6

September

Pingelhof in Alt Damerow, Mecklenburg-Vorpommern: Bis 1984 war der original erhaltene Bauernhof aus dem 17. Jh. in Familienbesitz. Danach wurde die Gemeinde Domsühl Eigentümer und gestaltete ihn zum agrarhistorischen Freilichtmuseum um.

Pingelhof in Alt Damerow, Mecklenburg-Western Pomerania. Until 1984, the 17th century farm in its original state was family property. Thereafter the parish of Domstühl took over ownership and turned it into an open air farming history museum.

7

September

Baggersee bei Bamberg, Bayern: Entlang des Mains reihen sich zahllose ehemalige Sandgruben aneinander, die voll Grundwasser liefen. Zwischen Bamberg und Schweinfurt, bei Trunstadt und Knetzgau, entstanden auf diese Weise großflächige Seen.

Man-made lake near Bamberg, Bavaria. Along the Main river, there are numerous former sandpits which have filled up with groundwater. Between Bamberg and Schweinfurt, near Trunstadt and Knetzgau, large lakes have formed in this way.

8

September

Bei Straubing, Bayern: 2850 Kilometer lang ist der Lauf der Donau von der Quelle im Schwarzwald bis zum Schwarzen Meer. Zwischen Regensburg und Passau hat der zweitgrößte Fluss Europas Platz zum Mäandern.

Near Straubing, Bavaria. The course of the Danube is 2850 kilometres long from its source in the Black Forest to the Black Sea. Between Regensburg and Passau, Europe's second largest river has scope to meander.

9

September

Schloss Herzberg, Niedersachsen: Seit rund 900 Jahren steht auf der Anhöhe über dem Ort Herzberg ein Schloss; vor 500 Jahren wurde dort die Sommerresidenz der Welfenherzöge errichtet. Die umliegenden Wälder und Wiesen gehören zum Naturpark Harz.

Herzberg Palace, Lower Saxony. A palace has stood on the hill above the town of Herzberg for around 900 years. 500 years ago, the summer residence of the Guelph dukes was built there. The surrounding forests and meadows belong to the Harz nature park.

10

September

Pfälzer Wald, Rheinland-Pfalz: Die Region ist das größte zusammenhängende Waldgebiet Deutschlands. 76 Prozent ihrer Fläche sind heute wieder von Wäldern bedeckt. Dies ist das Resultat von Aufforstungsbemühungen in den 1950er und 1960er Jahren.

Palatinate Forest, Rhineland-Palatinate. The region is the largest continuous stretch of forest in Germany. 76 percent of its area is once again covered with woodland. This is the result of reforestation projects in the 1950s and 60s.

11

September

Nationalpark Kellerwald, Hessen: Das Gebiet südlich des Ederstausees diente früher als fürstliches Jagdrevier und als Viehweide. Neben zahlreichen Laubbäumen finden sich auf den Ederhöhen und im Wildunger Bergland auch ein paar freie Wiesengründe.

Kellerwald National Park, Hesse. The area to the south of the Eder reservoir was formerly used as a baronial hunting ground and for cattle-grazing. As well as numerous deciduous trees, there are also a few areas of grassland on the Eder heights and the Wildung uplands.

12

September

Heißluftballons bei Lippstadt, Nordrhein-Westfalen: Eine Fahrt im Heißluftballon bietet ungewohnte Ausblicke auf Obstbäume in Reih und Glied und gleichmäßige Ackerfurchen, wie hier im Städtedreieck Lippstadt, Rheda-Wiedenbrück und Paderborn.

Hot-air balloons near Lippstadt, North Rhine-Westphalia. A trip in a hot-air balloon offers unusual perspectives on the fruit trees in Reih and Glied and on evenly ploughed furrows, seen here near the towns of Lippstadt, Rheda-Wiedenbrück and Paderborn.

13

September

Hermeskeil im Hunsrück, Rheinland-Pfalz: Die Flugausstellung L. + P. Junior zeigt über hundert Original-flugzeuge, darunter einen Lilienthal-Gleiter, die Super Constellation, mit der Konrad Adenauer 1955 nach Moskau flog, und eine Concorde.

Hermeskeil in the Hunsrück hills, Rhineland-Palatinate. The L.+P. Junior aviation museum exhibits over one hundred original aircraft including a Lilienthal Glider, the Super Constellation used by Konrad Adenauer for his flight to Moscow in 1955 and a Concorde.

14

September

Wolgast, Mecklenburg-Vorpommern: Die Peenewerft GmbH baut vor allem Containerschiffe. Einzelne Bauteile fertigt man in einer Halle vor; der Zusammenbau erfolgt in einem Trockendock im Freien. Anschließend lässt man das Schiff zu Wasser.

Wolgast, Mecklenburg-Western Pomerania. The Peenewerft GmbH shipyard builds mainly container ships. Individual parts are prefabricated in a factory and are then assembled in the open air dry dock. The ship is then launched.

15

September

Stadtzentrum, Hamburg: Mit 1,7 Millionen Einwohnern ist Hamburg die zweitgrößte Stadt Deutschlands. Im Zentrum zwischen Speicherstadt und Binnen- und Außenalster ragt die Turmruine von St. Nikolai als Kriegsmahnmal 147 m hoch aus dem Häusermeer.

City centre, Hamburg. With a population of 1.7 million, Hamburg is Germany's second largest city. The ruined tower of St Nikolai looms 147 m over the mass of houses as a war memorial in the city centre between the Speicherstadt and Binnen- and Außenalster districts.

16

September

Wertheim, Baden-Württemberg: Die Altstadt liegt auf dem Wörth, der dreieckigen Landzunge zwischen dem Main und der einmündenden Tauber. Zu Beginn des 12. Jhs. ließen die Grafen von Wertheim dort eine Burg errichten.

Wertheim, Baden-Württemberg. The old town is on the Wörth, the triangular stretch of land between the River Main and the River Tauber, which flows into it. At the beginning of the 12th century, the Counts of Wertheim had a castle built there.

17

September

Rothenburg, Bayern: Die schönste mittelalterliche Stadt Deutschlands blieb wohl nur so gut erhalten, weil sie abseits der großen Straßen lag. Hier musste nichts abgerissen werden, um Platz für eine wachsende Bevölkerung oder Industrie zu schaffen.

Rothenburg, Bavaria. Germany's most beautiful medieval town is so well-preserved because it lies off the beaten track. Nothing had to be demolished here to make space for a growing population or industry.

18

September

Kochelsee, Bayern: Der See ist im Lauf der Jahrhunderte stark verlandet. Stadt und Kloster Benediktbeuern standen im frühen Mittelalter an seinem Ufer; heute befinden sich sieben Kilometer zum Teil trockengelegte Moorlandschaft dazwischen.

Kochelsee, Bavaria. The lake has silted up considerably over the centuries. The town and monastery of Benediktbeuern stood on the banks of the lake during the early middle ages. Today seven kilometres of ɔartly dried up moorland separates them from the lake.

19

September

Kloster Ettal, Bayern: Ludwi[g] der Bayer (1281–1347) gründete das Kloster, um ein Gelübde zu erfüllen. »Ettal« leitet sich von »Ehe-Tal« ab: dem Bündnis des Kaisers mit Gott und der Jungfrau Maria. Beeindruckend: die Barockkuppe[l] der Kirche St. Maria.

Ettal Monastery, Bavaria. Louis the Bavarian (1281–134[7]) founded the monastery to fulf[il] a vow he had made. The nam[e] »Ettal« derives from »Ehe-Tal« (or valley of matrimony), whic[h] refers to the pact between the Emperor and God and the Virgin Mary. The baroque dom[e] of the Church of St Maria is most impressive.

20

September

Würzburg, Bayern: Die Ursprünge der Bischofs- und Universitätsstadt liegen auf dem Burgberg: Er trägt die Festung Marienberg, das Wahrzeichen der 125 000 Einwohner zählenden Stadt.

Würzburg, Bavaria. The origins of this episcopal and university city are found on the Burgberg mountain. The Marienberg fort, emblem of this city with its population of 125,000, sits atop it.

21

September

Hohenhameln, Niedersachsen: Auf dem hochwertigen Boden der Hildesheimer Börde werden hauptsächlich Weizen und Zuckerrüben angebaut. Die Praxis des Strohverbrennens ist heute nur noch in Ausnahmefällen und unter hohen Sicherheitsvorkehrungen erlaubt.

Hohenhameln, Lower Saxony. Mainly wheat and sugar beet are grown in the premium soil of the plains of the Hildesheimer Börde. The practice of burning straw is only permitted in exceptional circumstances nowadays and takes place under stringent safety precautions.

22

September

Weinbaugebiet am Main, Bayern: Seit mindestens 1200 Jahren bauen die Menschen in Mainfranken Wein an. Hier beleuchtet die Herbstsonne den flach gewölbten Rosenberg zwischen Nordheim und Sommerach.

Wine-growing area on the Main, Bavaria. Vines have been cultivated in Main-Franconia for at least 1200 years. Here, the autumn sun illuminates the gentle inclines of the Rosenberg between Nordheim and Sommerach.

23

September

Grasfeld bei Beelitz, Brandenburg: Zwei Landwirte in Wittbrietzen versorgen ihre Milchkühe mit frischem Ackergras, das sie auf einem runden Areal anbauen. Ihre Wassersprenganlage deckt eine Fläche von 670 Meter Durchmesser ab.

Grass field near Beelitz, Brandenburg. Two farmers in Wittbrietzen feed their dairy cows fresh couch grass which they grow on a round area of land. Their sprinkler system covers an area with a diamete of 670 metres.

24

September

Heißluftballons bei Volkach, Bayern: Beim Massenstart von den Mainwiesen erleuchten die Gasflammen die Ballonhüllen von innen. Einige der Luftfahrzeuge sind noch fest vertäut, damit sie nicht vorzeitig abheben, andere steigen bereits in die Höhe.

Hot-air balloons near Volkach, Bavaria. Gas flames illuminate the balloons from the inside at the mass lift-off from the meadows on the Main. Some are still firmly tethered, so they don't take off early, while others begin to soar away.

25

September

Die frühere DDR-Grenzanlage, Thüringen: 1378 Kilometer lang war die innerdeutsche Grenzanlage, die vom Fichtelgebirge über den Thüringer Wald, die Rhön und den Harz bis hinauf zur Lübecker Bucht Ost- und Westdeutschland teilte.

The former GDR border installations, Thuringia. The 1378 kilometre long inner German border, which divided East and West Germany, stretched from the Fichtel Mountains, via the Thuringian Forest, the Rhön and Harz areas, all the way up to Lübeck Bay.

26

September

Hopfenfelder, Bayern: In der Hallertau, auch Holledau genannt, wird seit tausend Jahren Hopfen kultiviert. Das größte Edelhopfenanbaugebiet der Erde zwischen Freising, Abensberg und Rottenburg liegt überwiegend in Niederbayern.

Hop fields, Bavaria. In the Hallertau area, also known as the Holledau, hops have been grown for a thousand years. The world's largest noble hops growing area lies predominantly in Lower Bavaria between Freising, Abensberg and Rottenburg.

27

September

Landschaftspark von Schloss Branitz, Brandenburg: Die Pyramide im See des Schlossparks birgt in einer Gruft die Begräbnisstätte von Hermann Fürst von Pückler-Muskau und seiner Gemahlin.

Branitz Palace country park, Brandenburg. The pyramid on the lake in the palace grounds contains the vaulted burial site of Prince Hermann von Pückler-Muskau and his wife.

28

September

Göltzschtalbrücke, Sachsen: Die 1846–1851 erbaute vierstöckige Eisenbahnbrücke auf der Strecke von Plauen nach Zwickau wurde seinerzeit als achtes Weltwunder bezeichnet: Der weltweit größte Bau dieser Art ist 78 m hoch und 574 m lang.

Göltzschtalbrücke, Saxony. The four-storey railway bridge – built between 1846 and 1851 on the route from Plauen to Zwickau – was described, at the time, as the eighth wonder of the world. It is the largest construction of its kind in the world and is 78 m high and 574 m long.

29

September

Breitenburger Moor, Schleswig-Holstein: Eine Hinterlassenschaft der Eiszeit in Norddeutschland ist die vielerorts von Mooren durchzogene Moränenlandschaft. Das Breitenburger Moor erstreckt sich südöstlich von Itzehoe bei der Ortschaft Breitenburg.

Breitenburg Moor, Schleswig-Holstein. A legacy of the ice age in northern Germany is the moraine landscape interspersed with moorland in many places. The Breitenburg Moor stretches south east of Itzehoe near the small town of Breitenburg.

30

September

Felder bei Xanten, Nordrhein-Westfalen: In den breiten Niederterrassen des Rheins hat auf fruchtbaren Böden die Landwirtschaft Raum. 15 n. Chr. gründeten die Römer etwas südlich des heutigen Xanten auf dem Fürstenberg ihr Castra Vetera.

Fields near Xanten, North Rhine-Westphalia. There is plenty of fertile farmland on the wide lower terraces of the Rhine. In the year 15 A.D., the Romans established Castra Vetera on the Fürstenberg, slightly to the south of what is now Xanten.

1

Oktober

Siegessäule, Berlin: Das 67 m hohe Denkmal, das an Preußens Siege gegen Dänemark 1864, Österreich 1866 und Frankreich 1870/71 erinnert, stand 1873–1938 vor dem Reichstag. Heute befindet es sich am Großen Stern, wo fünf Straßen aufeinandertreffen.

Victory Column, Berlin. The 67 m high monument, which commemorates Prussia's victories against Denmark in 1864, Austria in 1866 and France in 1870–71, stood from 1873 until 1938 in front of the Reichstag building. Today it is to be found on the Großer Stern, where five streets converge.

2

October

Kaiser-Wilhelm-Gedächtniskirche, Berlin: 1943 fiel dieses heutige Wahrzeichen Berlins einem Bombenangriff zum Opfer. Plänen, den alten Turmstumpf abzureißen, erteilten die Berliner Bürger eine Absage. Die Ruine wurde deshalb in den Neubau integriert.

Kaiser Wilhelm Memorial Church, Berlin. In 1943, this modern-day emblem of Berlin was hit by a bomb. Berlin's residents rejected plans to pull down the base of the old tower, so the ruins were integrated into the new building.

3

Oktober

Brandenburger Tor, Berlin: Als Deutschland noch geteilt war, konnte man das Brandenburger Tor vom Westen her nicht erreichen. Seit dem Mauerbau am 13. August 1961 symbolisierte es die Zweiteilung der Stadt.

Brandenburg Gate, Berlin. When Germany was still divided, it wasn't possible to approach the Brandenburg Gate from the west. After the wall was built on the 13th August 1961, it symbolised the division of the city.

4

October

Brandenburger Tor, Berlin: Friedrich Wilhelm II. ließ den klassizistischen Sandsteinbau 1788–1791 nach Entwürfen von Carl Gotthard Langhans erbauen. Die Quadriga von Johann Gottfried Schadow führte der Potsdamer Kupferschmied Emanuel Jury aus.

Brandenburg Gate, Berlin. Frederick William II had the neo-classical sandstone construction built between 1788 and 1791 based on the designs of Carl Gotthard Langhans. The quadriga, designed by Johann Gottfried Schadow, was made by the Potsdam coppersmith Emanuel Jury.

5

Oktober

Reichstag, Berlin: Bevor die Bundesregierung von Bonn nach Berlin umzog, durfte das Künstlerpaar Christo und Jeanne-Claude den Reichstag zwei Wochen lang verhüllen. 100 000 m^2 Polypropylengewebe und 15 600 m Seil waren dafür nötig.

Reichstag, Berlin. Before the government moved from Bonn to Berlin, the artist couple Christo and Jeanne-Claude was permitted to wrap the Reichstag for two weeks. This required 100,000 square metres of polypropylene fabric and 15,600 m of rope.

6

October

Reichstag, Berlin: Das Reichstagsgebäude – hier vor dem Umbau – ist heute wieder Sitz des deutschen Parlaments. 1894 von Paul Wallot errichtet, wurde es 1933 durch Brandstiftung schwer beschädigt und im Zweiten Weltkrieg zerstört.

Reichstag, Berlin. The Reichstag building – shown here before it was renovated – is now once again the seat of the German parliament. It was designed by Paul Wallot in 1894, sustained serious arson damage in 1933 and was destroyed in the Second World War.

7

Oktober

Schwerin, Mecklenburg-Vorpommern: Die mit 100 000 Einwohnern kleinste Hauptstadt eines Bundeslandes liegt am Rand der Mecklenburgischen Seenplatte. Sie ist von sieben Gewässern umgeben, Burgteich und Pfaffenteich erstrecken sich bis ins Zentrum.

Schwerin, Mecklenburg-Western Pomerania. Germany's smallest federal capital city – with 100,000 residents – lies on the edge of the Mecklenburg lake district. It is surrounded by seven bodies of water, of which the Burgteich and Pfaffenteich extend as far as the city centre.

8

October

Residenzschloss Schwerin, Mecklenburg-Vorpommern: 1857 wurde die Renaissanceanlage aus dem 16. Jh. im Neorenaissancestil modernisiert. Heute ist darin der Landtag des Bundeslandes Mecklenburg-Vorpommern untergebracht.

Schwerin Residenz Palace, Mecklenburg-Western Pomerania. In 1857, the Renaissance complex dating back to the 16th century was modernised in neo-Renaissance style. Today it is home to Mecklenburg-Western Pomerania's government.

9

Oktober

Die Nordsee: Über dem Meer verdunstet Wasser und steigt auf. Es bilden sich Wolken, die übers Land ziehen und abregnen. Die Flüsse bringen das Wasser zurück ins Meer – ein ewiger Kreislauf.

The North Sea. Water evaporates over the sea and rises. Clouds form, which drift over the country and turn to rain. The rivers return the water to the sea in a never-ending cycle.

10

October

Sandwatt bei Wangerooge, Niedersachsen: Zwischen der östlichsten der Ostfriesischen Inseln und dem Festland fällt der Meeresgrund bei Ebbe trocken. Trotzdem kann man Wangerooge nicht übers Watt erwandern, da tiefe Rinnen den Weg unterbrechen.

Sand flats near Wangerooge, Lower Saxony. At low tide, the seabed between this easternmost East Friesian Island and the mainland is exposed. However, you can't walk over the sand flats to Wangerooge due to deep trenches in the surface.

11

Oktober

Deutsche Bucht, Schleswig-Holstein: Das Sandwatt Gelbsand liegt am Rande der Elbmündung. Wie das ganze Wattenmeer zeichnet es sich durch eine große Artenvielfalt aus. Es ist dicht besiedelt von Muscheln, Wattwürmern, Schnecken und Krebsen.

German Bight, Schleswig-Holstein. The Gelbsand sand flats lie at the edge of the Elbe estuary. Like the rest of the Wadden Sea, the sand flats provide the habitat for a great diversity of species. They are densely populated by mussels, lugworms, snails and crabs.

12

October

Duhner Watt, Niedersachsen: Vom Steilsand bei Cuxhaven fließt das Wasser bei Ebbe in die Elbe, deren Mündungstrichter sich wenig weiter vollständig in die Nordsee öffnet. Das Duhner Watt ist Teil des Nationalparks Niedersächsisches Wattenmeer.

The Duhner mud flats, Lower Saxony. At low tide, water flows from Steilsand near Cuxhaven into the River Elbe. A short distance away, the Elbe's estuary opens into the North Sea. The Duhner mud flats belong to the Wadden Sea National Park of Lower Saxony.

13

Oktober

Elbe bei Glückstadt, Schleswig-Holstein: In Glückstadt, heißt es, gibt es die besten Matjesheringe. Seit 1968 werden an jedem dritten Donnerstag im Juni die »Glückstädter Matjeswochen« eröffnet. Die Heringe stammen aus der Nordsee.

The Elbe near Glückstadt, Schleswig-Holstein. It is said that Glückstadt has the best »Matjesheringe« or white herring. Since 1968 the »Glückstadt White Herring Weeks« have been opened on the third Thursday in June. The herring come from the North Sea.

14

October

Fehmarnsundbrücke, Schleswig-Holstein: Die 934 m lange Stahl- und Betonkonstruktion verbindet Fehmarn mit dem Festland. Da die Fahrbahn mit Drahtseilen an zwei geschwungenen Stahlträgern befestigt ist, wird die Brücke auch »Kleiderbügel« genannt.

The Fehmarn Sound Bridge, Schleswig-Holstein. The 934 m long steel and concrete construction connects Fehmarn with the mainland. Because the carriageway is attached with wire ropes to two curved steel girders, the bridge is also called the »clothes hanger«.

15

Oktober

Schloss Zwingenberg, Baden-Württemberg: Der Bergfried und die mächtige Schildmauer thronen schon seit dem 13. Jh. über der Neckarschleife. 1363 wurde die Burg geschleift. Nach dem Wiederaufbau zu Beginn des 14. Jh. wurde sie nie wieder erobert.

Zwingenberg Palace, Baden-Württemberg. The keep and the mighty protective wall have towered over the bend in the River Neckar since the 13th century. The castle was razed to the ground in 1363. After its reconstruction at the beginning of the 15th century, it was never captured again.

16

October

Kapelle bei Blaubeuren, Baden-Württemberg: Hier, am Südrand der mittleren Schwäbischen Alb, lebten schon vor rund 30 000 Jahren Menschen als Jäger und Sammler, was durch Funde von geschnitztem Mammutelfenbein belegt ist.

Chapel near Blaubeuren, Baden-Württemberg. Here, on the southern edge of the mid-Swabian Alb, humans lived as far back as 30,000 years ago as hunter-gatherers, as has been proven by discoveries of carved mammoth tusks.

17

Oktober

Feldberg, Baden-Württemberg: Die drei Gipfel und zwei Hochebenen bilden eine subalpine Insel im Schwarzwald. In der von der Eiszeit geformten Landschaft hat sich eine alpine Vegetation erhalten: Alpen-Löwenzahn, Gelber Enzian und Silberdistel.

Feldberg, Baden-Württemberg. The three summits and two high plains form a sub-alpine island in the Black Forest. The landscape was formed by the ice age and an alpine vegetation – featuring alpine dandelion, yellow gentian and Carline thistle – still exists today.

18

October

Schloss Schwetzingen, Baden-Württemberg: Den Schlossgarten ließ Kurfürst Carl Theodor im 18. Jh. nach dem Vorbild von Versailles errichten. Er besteht aus einem symmetrisch angelegten französischen Barockgarten und einem englischen Landschaftsgarten.

Schwetzingen Palace, Baden-Württemberg. In the 18th century Elector Charles Theodore had the palace gardens modelled on Versailles. They comprise a symmetrically designed French baroque garden and an English landscape garden.

19

Oktober

Schloss Moritzburg, Sachsen: Das Jagdhaus, das Herzog Moritz um 1545 im Friedewald bei Dresden bauen ließ, erweiterten seine Nachfolger zum prachtvollen Jagdschloss. Der heutige, im sächsischen Barockstil errichtete Bau entstand von 1723 bis 1736.

Moritzburg Palace, Saxony. The hunting lodge, which was built in the Friedewald forest near Dresden by Duke Moritz around 1545, was extended by his successors to a far grander affair. Today's building, in Saxon baroque style, was built between 1723 and 1736.

20

October

Teich bei Schloss Moritzburg, Sachsen: In einem der abgelassenen Teiche hat sich der erste Reif gebildet. Sächsische Adelsherren ließen ab dem 15. Jh. im flachen, sumpfigen Promnitztal Fischteiche anlegen, in denen bis heute Karpfen gezüchtet werden.

Pond near Moritzburg Palace, Saxony. The first frost has formed on one of the drained ponds. From the 15th century, Saxon noblemen had fish ponds constructed in the flat, marshy Promnitz valley, in which – to this day – carp are farmed.

21

Oktober

Grunewald, Berlin: Mehrere Naturschutzgebiete mit 111 Hektar Fläche gehören zu diesem ehemaligen Jagdrevier des preußischen Herrscherhauses. Ausflugsziel der Berliner wurde der Grunewald erst Ende des 19. Jhs., als er noch »Spandauer Forst« hieß.

Grunewald, Berlin. Several nature conservation areas – 111 hectares in size – form part of this former hunting ground of the Prussian rulers. Grunewald only became an excursion destination for the people of Berlin at the end of the 19th century, when it was still called the »Spandau Forest«.

22

October

Bei Coesfeld, Nordrhein-Westfalen: Wenn der Herbst beginnt, verfärben sich die Blätter der heimischen Laubbäume. Das Chlorophyll (Blattgrün) verschwindet aus den Blättern, die gelben und roten Farbstoffe bleiben zurück.

Near Coesfeld, North Rhine-Westphalia. When autumn begins, the leaves of the native deciduous trees change colour. The chlorophyll disappears from the leaves and the yellow and red pigments remain.

23

Oktober

Hafenanlage, Hamburg: Das Gelände des Hafens misst fast hundert Quadratkilometer. An den Kais haben 500 Seeschiffe gleichzeitig Platz. Jährlich löschen über 12 000 Schiffe hier ihre Ladung, was sechzig Millionen Tonnen Güterumschlag bedeutet.

Port facility, Hamburg. The port area measures almost one hundred square kilometres. There is space for 500 ocean-going vessels on the quayside at the same time. Each year over 12,000 ships offload their freight here, which involves sixty million tonnes of cargo handling.

24

October

Hafenanlage, Hamburg: Seit dem 12. Jh. können Seeschiffe diesen offenen Tidehafen trotz eines Gezeitenhubs von fast drei Metern auch bei Niedrigwasser anlaufen. 33 der insgesamt 60 Hafenbecken sind tief genug für Seeschiffe.

Port facility, Hamburg. Since the 12th century ocean-going vessels have been able to use this open tidal harbour even at low tide, despite a tidal rise of almost three metres. 33 of the 60 docks in total are deep enough for ocean-going ships.

25

Oktober

Wismar, Mecklenburg-Vorpommern: Die heutige Industrie- und Handelsstadt ging aus einer kurz vor 1200 gegründeten Siedlung an der Handelsstraße von Lübeck ins Baltikum hervor. Das Stadtrecht kam 1229. 1358 trat Wismar der Hanse bei.

Wismar, Mecklenburg-Western Pomerania. Today's industry and trade town dates back to a settlement established just before 1200 on the trade route from Lübeck to the Baltic States. It received its town charter in 1229 and joined the Hanseatic League in 1358.

26

October

Hebebrücke bei Wolgast, Mecklenburg-Vorpommern: Die Klappbrücke, die den Peenestrom überquert, verbindet die Bundesstraße 111 und die Eisenbahnlinie der Usedomer Bäder-Bahn mit Usedom. Deutschlands zweitgrößte Insel gilt als »Badewanne der Berliner«.

Lifting bridge near Wolgast, Mecklenburg-Western Pomerania. The bascule bridge over the Peenestrom strait connects the 111 main road and the Usedomer Bäder-Bahn railway with the island of Usedom. Germany's second largest island is referred to as the »Berliners' bathtub«.

27

Oktober

Wiehengebirge, Nordrhein-Westfalen: Der nördlichste Vorsprung der deutschen Mittelgebirgsschwelle erstreckt sich als etwa 10 km breiter und 60 km langer Höhenzug zwischen Osnabrück und Porta Westfalica.

Wiehen hills, North Rhine-Westphalia. This most northerly section of the German low level mountains is approximately 10 km wide and 60 km long and stretches from Osnabrück to Porta Westfalica.

28

October

Hochsauerland, Nordrhein-Westfalen: Ein Flug über das Rothaargebirge zeigt den Charakter dieses waldreichsten deutschen Gebirgszuges: 800 Meter hohe Bergkuppen, tief eingeschnittene Täler, gelegentlich Wiesen, Heiden, Moore und – vor allem Bäume.

Hochsauerland, North Rhine-Westphalia. A flight over the Rothaar mountains reveals the nature of this most wooded of German mountain ranges: namely 800 m high summits with deep-cut valleys, occasional meadows, heath and moorlands and an abundance of trees.

29

Oktober

Osterseen, Bayern: Zum Naturschutzgebiet Osterseen südlich des Starnberger Sees gehören 21 wassergefüllte, moorige Mulden, die noch Relikte aus der Eiszeit sind. Das Farbenspiel an den Seeufern geht auf den kalkhaltigen Untergrund zurück.

Osterseen, Bavaria. 21 water-filled, boggy depressions – left over from the ice age – are part of the Osterseen nature conservation area to the south of the Starnberg Lake. The play of colours on the banks of the lake is due to the calciferous bedrock.

30

October

Schloss Neuschwanstein, Bayern: »Märchenkönig« Ludwig II. träumte schon als Jugendlicher von der Nachbildung einer mittelalterlichen Burg auf einem Felsen über der Pöllat-Schlucht. 1869 begann er mit dem Bau, doch er starb 1886 vor der Vollendung.

Neuschwanstein Palace, Bavaria. Even as a boy, the »fairytale king« Louis II dreamt of making a replica of a medieval castle on a rock above the Pöllat gorge. In 1869 construction began but he died in 1886 before it was completed.

31

Oktober

Alpen, Bayern: In Deutschland liegt nur ein kleiner Teil der Alpen. Ein schmaler Streifen von Bergzügen zieht sich vom Bodensee im Westen bis zum Königssee im Osten. Sie gehören zu den Nördlichen Kalkalpen.

The Alps, Bavaria. Only a small section of the Alps lies in Germany. A narrow band of mountains stretches from Lake Constance in the west to the Königssee in the east. They are part of the Northern Limestone Alps.

1

November

Zugspitze, Bayern: Als Erstbesteiger des höchsten deutschen Berges (2962 m) gilt der bayerische Leutnant Karl Naus, der 1820 anlässlich von Vermessungsarbeiten den Gipfel betrat. Im Jahr 1897 entstand am Westgipfel das Münchner Haus des Alpenvereins.

Zugspitze, Bavaria. The Bavarian Lieutenant Karl Naus is accredited as the first person to climb Germany's highest mountain (2962 metres), after he reached the summit in 1820 while conducting surveying work. In the year 1897, the Alpine Club's »Munich House« was built on the western summit.

2

November

Walchensee, Bayern: Zwischen dem Herzogstand (links, 1731 m) und dem Jochberg (1567 m) zieht Nebel vom Walchensee nach Norden hinaus ins oberbayerische Voralpenland.

Walchensee, Bavaria. Between the Herzogstand (on the left, 1731 m) and the Jochberg (1567 m), fog drifts northwards from the Walchensee into the Upper Bavarian alpine upland.

3

November

Walchensee, Bayern: Die Insel Sassau darf von Menschen nicht betreten werden. 500-jährige Eiben und andere seltene Pflanzen wachsen dort. Alten Erzählungen nach soll auch der See Raritäten bergen: geheimnisvolle Gegenstände und Schätze.

Walchensee, Bavaria. People are not allowed onto the island of Sassau. 500 year old yew trees and other rare plants grow there. Legend has it that the lake holds other curiosities – mysterious objects and treasures.

4

November

Main bei Wertheim, Baden-Württemberg: Flussabwärts von Marktheidenfeld pendelt der Main zwischen Odenwald und Spessart, zwischen Schenkenwald und Hasselberger Wald hin und her. Die bayerisch-baden-württembergische Grenze verläuft in der Flussmitte.

River Main near Wertheim, Baden-Württemberg. Downriver from Marktheidenfeld, the Main winds to and fro between the Oden Forest and the Spessart Mountains, between the Schenken and Hasselberger Forests. The border between Baden-Württemberg and Bavaria runs along the middle of the river.

5

November

Steigerwald, Bayern: Hier zieht eine Haufenwolke über den Steigerwald bei Castell. Weiter südlich scheint die Sonne. Haufenwolken bauen sich bis zu einer Höhe von 5000 Metern auf.

Steiger Forest, Bavaria. A cumulus cloud formation is closing over the Steiger Forest at Castell. Further south the sun is shining. Cumulus clouds can form to a height of 5000 metres.

6

November

Langeoog, Niedersachsen: Bei einer schweren Sturmflut an Weihnachten 1717 brachen die Randdünen der Insel am großen und kleinen Schlopp, und sie zerteilte sich. Im Hintergrund sind zwei weitere Ostfriesische Inseln zu sehen: Baltrum und Norderney.

Langeoog, Lower Saxony. A major storm tide at Christmas 1717 caused the dunes on edge of the island at the large and small Schlopp to disintegrate and the island broke into pieces. In the background, two further East Friesian islands can be seen – Baltrum and Norderney.

7

November

Hafen im Alfsee bei Alfhausen, Niedersachsen: Die mit einem maximalen Stauinhalt von zwanzig Millionen Kubikmeter Wasser größte Hochwasserspeicheranlage Niedersachsens liegt zwischen den Städten Bersenbrück und Bramsche.

Harbour on the Alfsee near Alfhausen, Lower Saxony. The biggest flood storage reservoir in Lower Saxony, with a maximum capacity of twenty million cubic metres, is situated between the towns of Bersenbrück and Bramsche.

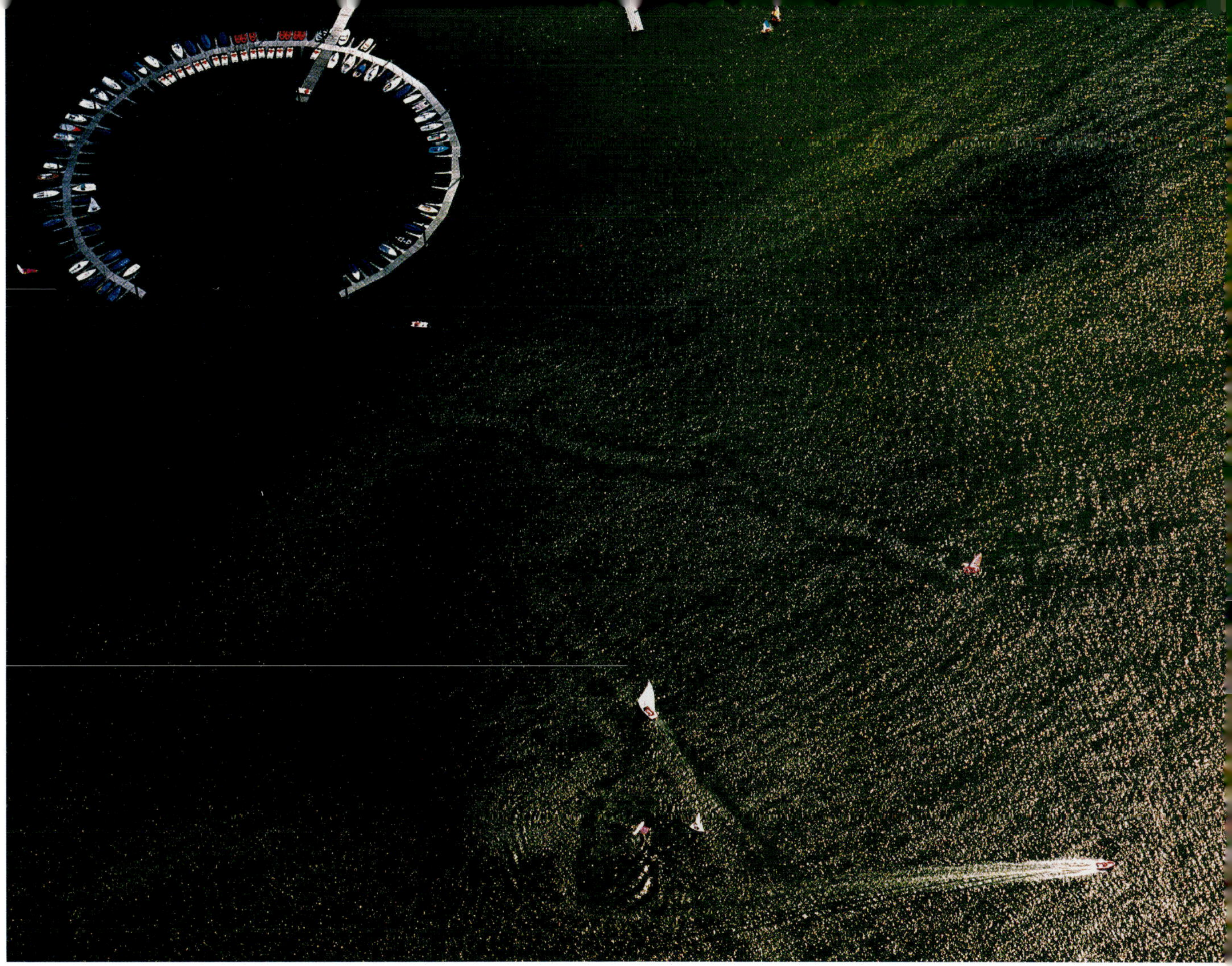

8

November

Karpfenteiche bei Herzogen-
aurach, Bayern: Ungefähr
11 000 Tonnen Karpfen
produzieren die deutschen
Teichwirte pro Jahr. Etwa
zwanzig Prozent der Fische
wachsen in der mittel-
fränkischen Teichland-
schaft heran.

*Carp ponds near Herzogen-
aurach, Bavaria. German fish
farmers produce around
11,000 tonnes of carp each year.
Around twenty percent of the
fish are reared in the pond
region of Central Franconia.*

9

November

Felder bei Vettweiß, Nordrhein-Westfalen: Gleich unterhalb des deutsch-belgischen Naturparks Hohes Venn in Richtung Kölner Bucht liegt die Zülpicher Börde. Zwischen Düren und Vettweiß wird die tonhaltige Braunerde landwirtschaftlich genutzt.

Fields near Vettweiß, North Rhine-Westphalia. The plains of the Zülpicher Börde lie just below the German-Belgian Hohes Venn Nature Park, towards the Cologne basin. The clayey brown soil is used for agriculture between Düren and Vettweiß.

10

November

Braunkohlekraftwerk Jänschwalde, Brandenburg: Das Kraftwerk liefert nicht nur Strom, es kommt gleichzeitig der Fischzucht Jänschwalde zugute. Diese nutzt das aufgeheizte Kühlwasser, um die Fische auch im Winter im Warmen zu halten.

Jänschwalde brown coal power station, Brandenburg. The power station does not just generate electricity. It also benefits the Jänschwalde fish farm, which uses the heated cooling water to keep the fish warm in winter.

11

November

Jena, Thüringen: Ein modernes Wahrzeichen ist der Intershop-Turm. Dahinter befindet sich ein Teil der Universitätsklinik. Nach der Wiedervereinigung entwickelte sich Jena zu einem Bildungs- und Wissenschaftszentrum mit über dreißig Instituten.

Jena, Thuringia. The Intershop Tower is a modern-day emblem of the city. Part of the University Hospital is situated behind it. After reunification, Jena developed into a centre of science and learning with over thirty institutes.

12

November

Rhön, Bayern: Auf dem höchsten Punkt des Farnsbergs, bei 786 Metern über dem Meeresspiegel, steht das Würzburger Karl-Straub-Haus. Der Rhönklub Würzburg erbaute es 1938 als Einkehr- und Übernachtungsmöglichkeit für Wanderer.

The Rhön, Bavaria. The Karl-Straub-Haus sits on the highest point of the Farnsberg (786 metres above sea level). It was constructed by the Würzburg branch of the Rhön Club in 1938 to provide refreshments and accommodation for hikers.

13

November

Feldberg, Baden-Württemberg: Mit 1493 Metern ist der Feldberg nicht nur der höchste Berg des Schwarzwalds, sondern aller deutschen Mittelgebirge. Sein Gipfelmassiv erstreckt sich über mehrere Kilometer.

Feldberg, Baden-Württemberg. At a height of 1493 metres, the Feldberg is not only the highest peak of the Black Forest, but of all German low mountain ranges. Its summit plateau is several kilometres long.

14

November

Kuppenrhön, Thüringen: Die Rhön gliedert sich in das Rhönvorland mit lang gestreckten Bergrücken, die Kuppenrhön mit kegelartigen Bergen vulkanischen Ursprungs und den massigen Bergzug der Hohen Rhön im Zentrum der Vulkanlandschaft.

Kuppenrhön, Thuringia. The Rhön area splits into the Rhönvorland with its elongated ridge, the Kuppenrhön with cone-shaped mountains of volcanic origin and the huge ridge of the Hoher Rhön in the middle of the volcanic landscape.

15

November

Bei Schwabmünchen, Bayern: Ein Feuchtbiotop im Naherholungsgebiet Stauden ist winterbedingt trockengefallen. Es liegt im Süden des »Naturparks Augsburg-Westliche Wälder«.

Near Schwabmünchen, Bavaria. A wetland habitat in the local recreation area of Stauden has dried out due to winter. It lies in the south of the »Naturpark Augsburg-Westliche Wälder«.

16

November

Schwarzwald, Baden-Württemberg: Der Schwarzwald bildete einst mit den Vogesen ein zusammenhängendes Gebirge. Seit dem Einbruch des Oberrheingrabens – beginnend vor etwa sechzig Millionen Jahren – sind die Mittelgebirge getrennt.

Black Forest, Baden-Württemberg. The Black Forest and the Vosges mountains used to form one continuous mountain range. Since the Upper Rhine Rift formed – starting some sixty million years ago – the low mountain ranges have been separate.

17

November

Der Bayerische Wald bei Deggendorf, Bayern: Auf einer Höhe von etwa 400 m steigt der Vordere Bayerische Wald aus dem fruchtbaren Gäuboden empor. Die Gipfel sind 700–1100 m hoch. Insgesamt zählt das Gebirge 132 Berge von über tausend Meter Höhe.

Bavarian Forest near Deggendorf, Bavaria. At around 400 m above sea level, the front hills of the Bavarian Forest rise up from the fertile Gäuboden area. The peaks are 700–1100 m high. There are, in total, 132 mountains of over one thousand metres in the range.

18

November

Riedenburg, Bayern:
Über Riedenburg und dem Schambachtal liegt Schloss Rosenburg, wo Falkner die Flugkunst ihrer Greifvögel zeigen. In den 90er-Jahren wurde die Altmühl, die durch Riedenburg fließt, ausgebaut und in den Main-Donau-Kanal integriert.

Riedenburg, Bavaria. Rosenburg Palace, where falconers demonstrate the flying skills of their birds of prey, is situated above Riedenburg and the Schambach valley. In the 1990s, the Altmühl river, which flows through Riedenburg, was widened and incorporated into the Main-Danube Canal.

19

November

Parsberg, Bayern: Das Wechselspiel von Aufbau und kriegerischer Zerstörung blieb auch der Parsberger Burg im Laufe ihrer Geschichte nicht erspart. Die letzte Version entstand Mitte des 17. Jhs. nach dem Dreißigjährigen Krieg.

Parsberg, Bavaria. Parsberg Castle has a chequered history of wartime destruction and subsequent reconstruction. The current castle was built in the middle of the 17th century, after the Thirty Years' War.

20

November

Das Nebelhorn, Bayern: Mit einer Kabinenbahn schweben Skifahrer von Oberstdorf aus auf einer 5 km langen Fahrtstrecke nach oben. Schlepp- und Sessellifte erschließen den Gipfel, von dem aus die längste Skipiste Deutschlands (7,5 km) ins Tal führt.

The Nebelhorn, Bavaria. Skiers are carried 5 km up the mountain by cable car from Oberstdorf. Draglifts and chairlifts continue to the summit, where Germany's longest ski run of 7.5 km leads back down to the valley.

21

November

Hummeratsried, Bayern: Die Wertach sammelt einen Großteil ihres Wassers in den Niederungen bei Marktoberdorf. Der Boden ist moorig. Birken, Grauerlen und gelegentlich Weiden und Pappeln stehen in Gruppen.

Hummeratsried, Bavaria. The Wertach river gathers a large part of its water in the lowlands near Marktoberdorf. The ground is boggy. Birches, grey alder and occasional willows and poplars stand in groups.

22

November

Bei Sonthofen, Bayern: Zwischen den Dörfern Tiefenberg und Altstädten fließt der Iller-Zufluss Leybach durch den Wiesengrund »Im Moos«. Am Rand der Weiden stehen die Heustadel, die das Landschaftsbild der Region mit prägen.

Near Sonthofen, Bavaria. The Leybach, a tributary of the Iller, flows between the villages of Tiefenberg and Altstädten through the meadows of »Im Moos«. The hay sheds, which characterise the region's landscape, stand on the edge of the fields.

23

November

Das Donauried, Bayern: Die völlig ebene Moor- und Auenlandschaft erstreckt sich längs der Donau von Ulm bis Neuburg. Mit der Ansiedlung der Alemannen begann die Kultivierung des Moorbodens als Ackerland.

Donauried, Bavaria. This totally flat area of moorland and water meadows stretches along the Danube from Ulm to Neuburg. The settlement of the Alemanni heralded the cultivation of the boggy soil for arable land.

24

November

Wiesenttal, Bayern: Soeben noch wand sich die Wiesent in heftigen Schlingen durch die Fränkische Schweiz, doch hier, vor Forchheim und der Mündung in die Regnitz, lässt das Gefälle nach, und der Fluss beruhigt sich.

Wiesent Valley, Bavaria. Just a short way away the Wiesent river was twisting and turning through the Franconian Switzerland area, yet here, outside Forchheim before the river flows into the Regnitz, the slope eases off and the river levels out.

Lichtung Ödwies, Bayern: Die Wiese, auf der Kammhöhe des Bayerischen Waldes in über 1000 m Höhe gelegen, rodeten Bauern Mitte des 16. Jhs. Heute befinden sich dort ein Forsthaus und eine Kapelle.

Ödwies Clearing, Bavaria. The meadow, on the ridge of the Bavarian Forest at over 1000 m above sea level, was cleared by farmers in the middle of the 16th century. Today a forester's house and a chapel stand there.

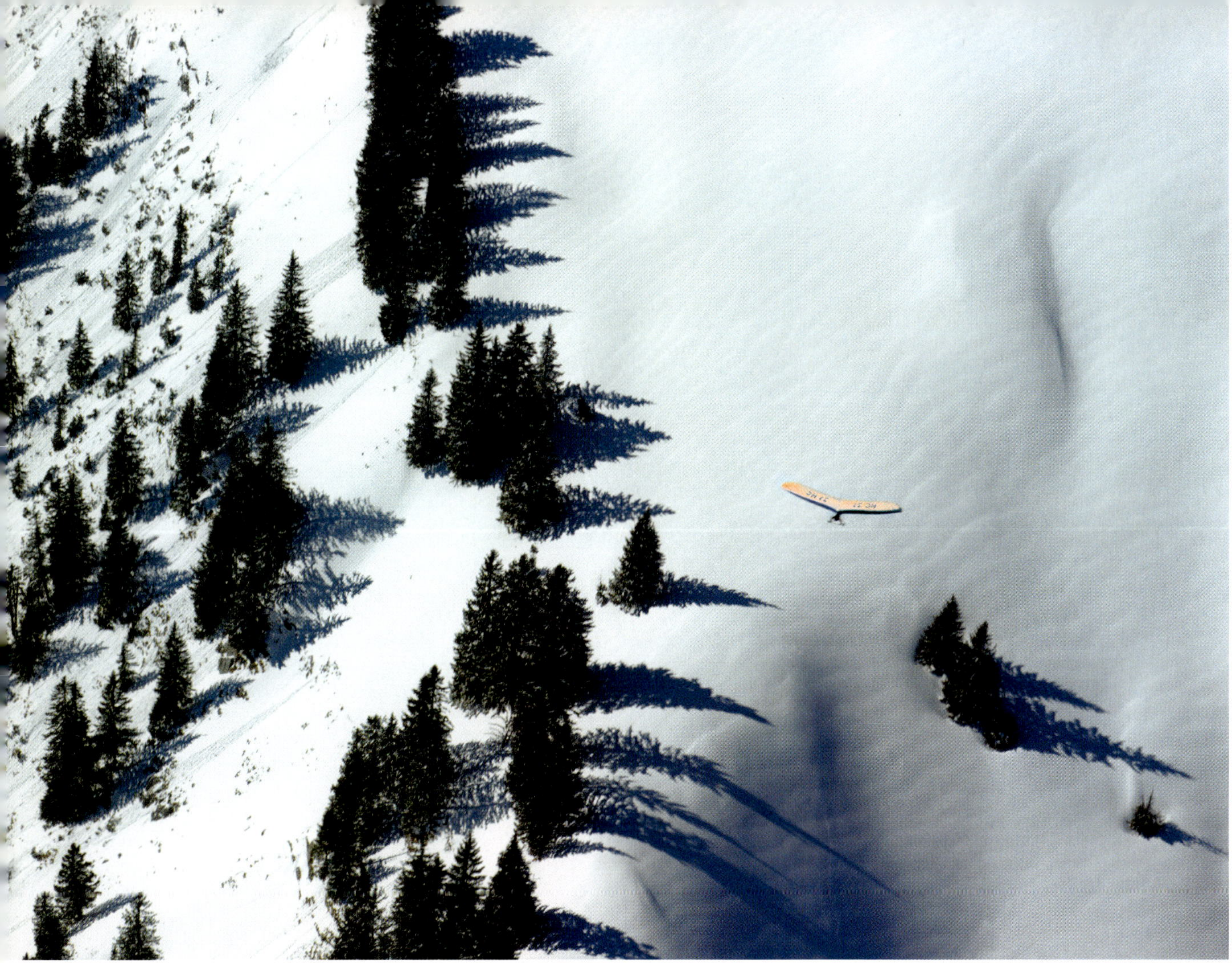

26

November

Nationalpark Berchtesgaden, Bayern: Der einzige deutsche Nationalpark der Alpen wurde 1978 eingerichtet. 1990 wies ihn die UNESCO als Biosphärenreservat aus. Das einzigartige Naturgebiet beherbergt viele Pflanzen, die sonst nicht mehr zu finden sind.

Berchtesgaden National Park, Bavaria. Germany's only alpine national park was established in 1978. In 1990, it was designated a UNESCO biosphere reserve. This unique habitat is home to many plants which are otherwise extinct.

27

November

Allgäu, Bayern: Am Rande der Skiarena Steibis bei Oberstaufen finden sich unpräparierte Hänge. Die einen nutzen sie zum alpinen Tiefschneefahren, die anderen für eine Skitour durch den unberührten Schnee.

Allgäu, Bavaria. Unprepared slopes are to be found on the edge of the Skiarena Steibis resort near Oberstaufen. Some people use them for alpine powder-snow skiing while others use them ski-touring in virgin snow.

28

November

Tegernsee-Schliersee-Gebiet, Bayern: Die Seenlandschaft bei Miesbach war einst Sitz der reichsunmittelbaren Herrschaft Hohenwaldeck. Erst nach dem Tod des letzten Maxlrainers fielen Miesbach und Umgebung 1734 an das damalige Kurfürstentum Bayern.

The Tegernsee and Schliersee region, Bavaria. This lakeland area near Miesbach used to be the seat of the county of Hohenwaldeck, which was under the suzerainty of the Holy Roman Empire. It was not until the death of the last of the Maxlrainers that Miesbach and its surroundings became part of the then Electorate of Bavaria in 1734.

29

November

Bei Rottach-Egern, Bayern: Die Ufer des Tegernsees sind fast rundum verbaut, die Orte Gmund, Bad Wiessee, Rottach-Egern und Tegernsee stark überlaufen. Doch nur wenig abseits herrscht noch die Natur.

Near Rottach-Egern, Bavaria. The banks of the Tegernsee are almost completely built up and the towns of Gmund, Bad Wiessee, Rottach-Egern and Tegernsee are bustling. Yet just a short way off the beaten track, nature rules.

30

November

Fichtelgebirge, Bayern: Vom Ochsenkopf aus reicht der Blick bis zu den Alpen. Er erfasst fünf Gebirgszüge, die Deutschland im Südosten begrenzen: Fichtelgebirge, Oberpfälzer Wald, Böhmerwald, Bayerischer Wald und Chiemgauer Alpen.

The Fichtelgebirge mountain range, Bavaria. From the summit of the Ochsenkopf you can see as far as the Alps. The view spans five mountain ranges which form the south-eastern German border, namely the Fichtelgebirge, the Upper Palatinate Forest, Bohemian Forest, Bavarian Forest and the Chiemgau Alps.

1

Dezember

Alpen, Bayern: Die ersten Bergsteiger waren Alphirten, Jäger, Botaniker und Landvermesser. Bergsteigen als Sport kam erst in den 1850er Jahren auf. Ab 1869 machte der Deutsche Alpenverein die Berge durch Wanderwege und Hütten allgemein zugänglich.

The Alps, Bavaria. The first mountaineers were alpine herdsmen, hunters, botanists and land surveyors. Mountaineering as a sport only emerged in the 1850s. From 1869 the German Alpine Club made the mountains more widely accessible through footpaths and mountain huts.

2

Dezember

Aischgrund, Bayern:
Gut 200 Kilometer liegen zwischen dem »Karpfenland« Aischgrund und den Alpen im Hintergrund. Unter dem Dunst verbergen sich die Hügelketten der Frankenhöhe und der Fränkischen Alb.

Aischgrund, Bavaria. It is a good 200 kilometres from the »carp country« of Aischgrund to the Alps in the background. Below the mist, the hills of the Franconian Heights and the Franconian Jura are hidden.

3

December

Chiemsee, Bayern: Die drei Inseln Frauenchiemsee, Krautinsel und Herrenchiemsee (von vorn nach hinten) entstanden in der letzten Eiszeit. Ihr geologischer Untergrund ist so hart, dass die Gletscher ihn weniger stark abschliffen als die Umgebung.

Chiemsee, Bavaria. The three islands of Frauenchiemsee, Krautinsel and Herrenschiemsee (from front to back) date back to the last ice age. Their bedrock is so hard that they were worn away less by glaciers than the surrounding area.

4

Dezember

Bei Frasdorf, Bayern: Zwischen Chiemsee und Simssee erstreckt sich bis zu den Chiemgauer Alpen ein typischer Ausschnitt aus der Voralpenlandschaft. Die leicht hügelige Landschaft bildete sich aus den Grundmoränen von Eiszeitgletschern.

Near Frasdorf, Bavaria. A typical section of landscape in the foothills of the Alps stretches from the Chiemsee and Simssee to the Chiemgau Alps. The gentle rolling countryside emerged from the ground moraines of the ice age glaciers.

5

December

Dammkar bei Mittenwald, Bayern: Immer mehr Skifahrer suchen ihren Spaß abseits der präparierten Pisten. Wenig Spaß haben dabei aufgeschreckte Wildtiere, die im Winter ohnehin am Limit leben: Die panische Flucht kann sie die letzten Reserven kosten.

Dammkar near Mittenwald, Bavaria. More and more skiers crave the thrill of going off-piste. It's not much fun for startled wild animals though, which struggle to survive the winter as it is. Taking flight in panic can cost them their last reserves of energy.

6

Dezember

Chiemgau, Bayern: Die Anfänge des Skifahrens reichen bis in die Jungsteinzeit zurück. In Skandinavien und Nordrussland wurden damals Gleithölzer zur Fortbewegung genutzt. Der Skisport wurde erst im 19. Jh. erfunden, die ersten Skilifte um 1930.

The Chiemgau region, Bavaria. The origins of skiing date back to the New Stone Age. At that time in Scandinavia and northern Russia, wooden planks were used as a means of transport. Skiing as a sport was only invented in the 19th century and the first ski lifts were introduced in the 1930s.

7

December

Kapelle bei Großried, Bayern: In der Nähe von Bad Wörishofen im Unterallgäu liegt die Gemeinde Großried. Die etwas außerhalb des Dorfes stehende klassizistische Kapelle Heilig-Kreuz-Erhöhung dient zugleich als Pfarrkirche.

Chapel near Großried, Bavaria. The parish of Großried is near Bad Wörishofen in the Unterallgäu area. The neoclassical Heilig-Kreuz-Erhöhung Chapel, which stands a little outside the village, is also the parish church.

8

Dezember

Walchensee, Bayern: Für die Herkunft des Namens »Walchensee« gibt es verschiedene Erklärungen: Er könnte auf den lateinischen Lacus vallensis (im Tal gelegener See) zurückgehen oder aber auf die Walchen oder Welschen (keltische und römische Siedler).

Walchensee, Bavaria. There are various possible explanations as to the meaning of the name »Walchensee«. It may derive from the Latin Lacus vallensis (a lake in the valley), or it may refer to the Walchen or Volcae (celtic and roman settlers).

9

December

Sylvensteinspeicher, Bayern: Seit 1959 reguliert der Stausee die Hochwasser der Isar. Beim Höchstwasserstand hält er 104 Millionen Kubikmeter. Er ähnelt dann einem Fjord und ist zwanzig Kilometer lang.

Sylvenstein Reservoir, Bavaria. Since 1959 the reservoir has regulated floods on the River Isar. It holds a maximum of 104 million cubic metres. When full, it resembles a fjord and is 20 kilometres long.

10

Dezember

Wattenmeer, Niedersachsen: Die Sandbank Itzendorfplate zwischen der Ostfriesischen Insel Juist und der Stadt Norden auf dem Festland gehört zum Nationalpark Niedersächsisches Wattenmeer.

Wadden Sea, Lower Saxony. The Itzendorfplate sandbank between the East Friesian island of Juist and the mainland town of Norden is part of the Wadden Sea National Park of Lower Saxony.

11

December

Stade, Niedersachsen: An der Niederelbe lagern Tausende von Baumstämmen. Das Wasser konserviert sie bis zum Weitertransport. Die Schwinge, ein Nebenfluss der Elbe, umfließt die Altstadt von Stade und strömt durch den Burggraben und den Floßhafen.

Stade, Lower Saxony. On the Lower Elbe river, thousands of tree trunks are stored, preserved in the water until their onward transport. The Schwinge is a tributary of the Elbe and encircles the old town of Stade, flowing through the moat and the raft port.

12

Dezember

Bei Höchstädt, Bayern: Infolge der Donaubegradigung und der Entwässerung der Landschaft verwandelten sich die einstigen Auwälder in Ackerland und Kiesgruben. Letztere nutzt man heute als Fischteiche.

Near Höchstädt, Bavaria. As a result of the straightening of the Danube and countryside drainage, the former alluvial forests have been transformed into fields and gravel pits. The latter are today used as fish ponds.

13

December

Neckar, Baden-Württemberg: Der Fluss hat sich auf seinem Weg zum Rhein in den Buntsandstein tief eingeschnitten und bildet bei Binau unweit von Mosbach eine Schleife. Im Dunst verborgen über dem Neckar liegt die Burgruine Dauchstein.

River Neckar, Baden-Württemberg. On its way to the Rhine, the river has cut a deep cleft into the new red sandstone and forms a loop near Binau, close to Mosbach. The ruined Dauchstein Castle is hidden in the mist above the Neckar.

14

Dezember

Der Rheinhafen von Karlsruhe, Baden-Württemberg: Der wirtschaftliche Aufschwung Karlsruhes begann 1901 mit der Eröffnung des Hafens im Stadtteil Daxlanden. Die Hafenbecken sind durch einen zwei Kilometer langen Stichkanal mit dem Rhein verbunden.

The port of Karlsruhe on the Rhine, Baden-Württemberg. The upturn in the economy of Karlsruhe began in 1901 with the opening of the port in the Daxlanden part of the city. The docks are connected to the Rhine by means of a two kilometre branch canal.

15

December

Der Ölhafen von Karlsruhe, Baden-Württemberg: In den Tanks lagern flüssige und gasförmige Mineralölprodukte der nahe gelegenen Raffinerie MiRO, die hier auf Tankschiffe verladen werden.

Oil port at Karlsruhe, Baden-Württemberg. The tanks carry liquid and gaseous oil products from the nearby MiRO refinery, which are loaded onto barges here.

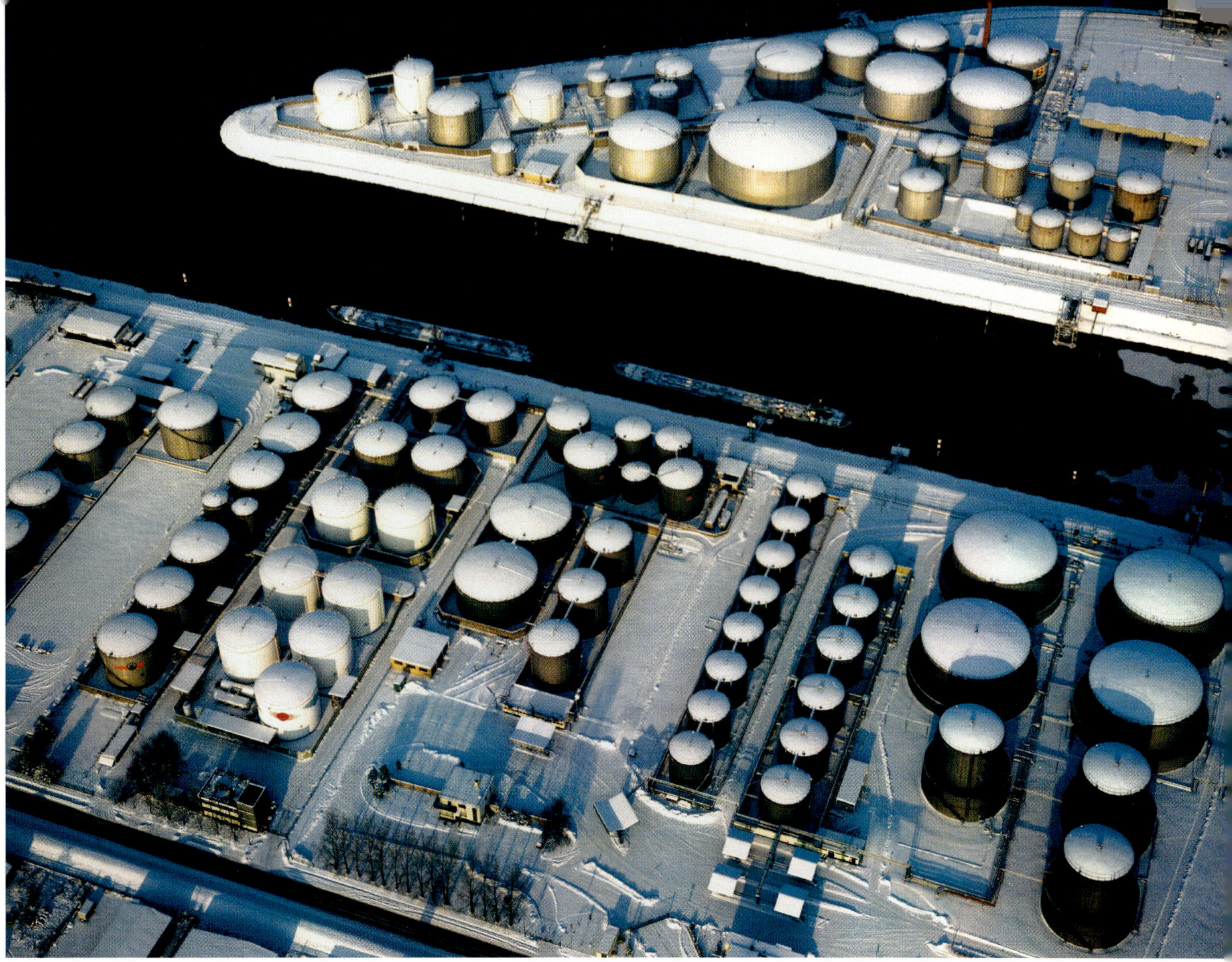

16

Dezember

Wolkendecke über Gundremmingen, Bayern: Der Dampf der Kühltürme des Kernkraftwerks Gundremmingen bei Günzburg durchdringt die ansonsten geschlossene Wolkendecke. Praktischer Nebeneffekt: Die Dampfwolken dienen Piloten als Orientierungshilfe.

Cloud cover over Gundremmingen, Bavaria. Steam from the cooling towers of the Gundremmingen nuclear power station near Günzburg breaches the otherwise completely overcast sky. One benefit of this – the steam is a handy orientation point for pilots.

17

December

Füssen, Bayern: Auf der Anhöhe stehen das 1697–1727 erbaute Benediktinerkloster St. Mang und die gleichnamige Stadtpfarrkirche. Sie wurde 1701–1717 über dem Grab des heiligen Magnus (»Sankt Mang«) errichtet.

Füssen, Bavaria. The Benedictine Monastery St Mang (built from 1697 to 1727), and the parish church of the same name, stand on the hill. The church was built from 1701 to 1717 above the grave of Saint Magnus (»Sankt Mang«).

18

Dezember

Schweindorf, Baden-Württemberg: Der 300 Einwohner zählende Ort liegt auf dem Härtsfeld in der Schwäbischen Alb zwischen Heidenheim und Nördlingen. Der Waldrand vorne ist zugleich die Landesgrenze zwischen Baden-Württemberg und Bayern.

Schweindorf, Baden-Württemberg. This 300-strong hamlet is situated on the Härtsfeld in the Swabian Alb mountains, between the towns of Heidenheim and Nördlingen. The front edge of the forest is the border between the federal states of Baden-Württemberg and Bavaria.

19

December

Abenheim, Rheinland-Pfalz: Allein auf weiter Flur, nahe der Landstraße nach Osthofen, steht die Abenheimer Kapelle. Die Ebene liegt nördlich von Worms auf einer Niederterrasse des Rheins. Die fruchtbare Erde ermöglicht intensiven Gemüseanbau.

Abenheim, Rhineland-Palatinate. Abenheim Chapel stands isolated on an expanse of farmland close to the country road towards Osthofen. The plain lies north of the city of Worms on a low-level terrace on the banks of the Rhine. The fertile land facilitates intensive market gardening.

20

Dezember

Winterberg, Nordrhein-Westfalen: Die Bob- und Rodelbahn an der Winterberger Kappe zählt zu den schnellsten der Welt. Die Fahrer erreichen hier Spitzengeschwindigkeiten von bis zu 150 Stundenkilometern.

Winterberg, North Rhine-Westphalia. The bobsleigh and toboggan run on the Winterberger Kappe is one of the fastest in the world. The crews reach top speeds of up to 150 kilometres per hour.

21

December

Loipen bei Schwangau, Bayern: Zwischen dem Bannwaldsee und dem Tegelberg hat der Winterdienst Loipen gespurt. Sie beginnen im heilklimatischen Luftkurort Schwangau und führen durch das Naturschutzgebiet Ammergauer Alpen.

Cross-country ski tracks near Schwangau, Bavaria. Between the Bannwaldsee and the Tegelberg, the ground has been prepared for cross-country skiing. The tracks start in the spa town of Schwangau and wind through the Ammergau Alps nature reserve.

22

Dezember

Bayerischer Wald, Bayern: Sieben Alpinskigebiete und sechs Langlaufgebiete wurden in der touristisch geprägten Region erschlossen. Schneesicherheit wird in Sankt Englmar ebenso garantiert wie am Großen Arber, Brotjacklriegel, Lusen oder Dreisessel.

Bavarian Forest, Bavaria. Seven alpine ski and six cross-country areas have been developed in this tourism focussed region. You are as sure of reliable snow conditions in Sankt Englmar as on the Großer Arber, Brotjacklriegel, Lusen or the Dreisessel.

23

December

Rachelkapelle, Bayerischer Wald: 1885 verirrte sich Forstmeister Ludwig Leythäuser im Nebel. Plötzlich weigerte sich sein Pferd weiterzugehen. Er stieg ab und sah vor sich den Abgrund der Rachelseewand. Zum Dank für die Rettung stiftete er die Kapelle.

Rachelkapelle, Bavarian Forest. In 1885, head forester Ludwig Leythäuser had lost his way in fog when his horse suddenly refused to go further. He dismounted and saw before him the edge of the precipice above Lake Rachel. He donated the chapel in gratitude at his narrow escape.

24

Dezember

Tannenbäume bei Sonthofen, Bayern: Nur 400 Jahre alt ist der Brauch, einen Christbaum aufzustellen. 1605 wird erstmals über geschmückte Tannenbäume in Straßburger Wohnungen berichtet. Im 19. Jh. leuchteten Christbaumkerzen weltweit in vielen Häusern.

Fir trees near Sonthofen, Bavaria. The custom of putting up a Christmas tree is only 400 years old. First reports of decorated fir trees in Strasbourg homes date back to 1605. In the 19th century Christmas tree candles were lit in many houses around the world.

25

December

Isartal zwischen Wallgau und Vorderriß, Bayern: Die Alpen bilden die Grenze zwischen Mittel- und Südeuropa. Sie sind das höchste Gebirge Europas und eine wichtige Klima- und Wetterscheide.

Isar valley between Wallgau and Vorderriss, Bavaria. The Alps form the boundary between central and southern Europe. It is the highest mountain range in Europe and an important climatic and meteorological divide.

26

Dezember

Söllereck, Bayern: Von Kornau bei Oberstdorf am Eingang ins Kleinwalsertal trägt eine Gondelbahn die Skifahrer hinauf auf das 1706 Meter hohe Söllereck.

Söllereck, Bavaria. At the mouth of the Kleinwalser valley a cable car transports skiers from Kornau, near Oberstdorf, up the 1706 m high Söllereck.

Almhütte bei Bad Hindelang, Bayern: Im Naturschutzgebiet Rettenbachtal rund um den Großen Daumen (2280 Meter) herrscht Winterruhe. Die Almhütte am Rotspitz bleibt verlassen, bis die Senner im Frühjahr wieder die Kühe auftreiben.

Mountain hut near Bad Hindelang, Bavaria. It's the dead of winter in the Rettenbachtal nature reserve at the Großer Daumen (2280 m). The mountain hut on the Rotspitz lies empty until spring, when the dairy farmers drive their herds back up the mountain.

28

Dezember

Loisach-Isar-Kanal bei Wolfratshausen, Bayern: Der um 1900 geschaffene Kanal gehört zum System der Stromgewinnung mittels Wasserkraft. Er leitet Wasser aus der Loisach in die Isar um, wo insgesamt 23 Laufwasserkraftwerke installiert sind.

Loisach-Isar Canal near Wolfratshausen, Bavaria. The canal, which was built around 1900, is part of a system for generating electricity using water power. It diverts water from the River Loisach into the River Isar, where a total of 23 hydroelectric power stations are installed.

29

December

Kloster Paring, Bayern: Langquaid an der Großen Laaber ist von Wäldern und Feldern umgeben. Die Religiosität der Menschen hat in dieser Gegend ihre Spuren hinterlassen: Es gibt eine Vielzahl von Kirchen, Klöstern und Wallfahrtskirchen.

Paring Monastery, Bavaria. Langquaid on the Großer Laaber river is surrounded by forests and fields. The religiousness of the people has left its mark on the region with its many churches, monasteries and pilgrimage chapels.

30

Dezember

Zugspitze, Bayern: Deutschlands höchsten Gipfel können auch Nichtbergsteiger ohne Anstrengung erklimmen: Von Grainau und von Ehrwald (in Tirol) führen Seilbahnen hinauf, von Garmisch-Partenkirchen über Eibsee und Grainau eine Zahnradbahn.

Zugspitze, Bavaria. Even non-mountaineers can scale Germany's highest peak without much effort. From Grainau and from Ehrwald (in the Austrian Tyrol), cable cars lead to the top. From Garmisch-Partenkirchen, a cog railway ascends via Eibsee and Grainau.

31

December

Die Alpen, Bayern: Wie alle Gebirge sind auch die Alpen durch die Drift der Kontinentalplatten entstanden. Vor rund 50 Millionen Jahren schob sich die Afrikanische Platte nordwärts über die Eurasische. Dabei falteten sich hohe Berge auf.

The Bavarian Alps. As with all mountain ranges, the Alps were created by the drift of the earth's tectonic plates. Around 50 million years ago, the African plate moved northwards over the Eurasian plate, causing the formation of high mountains.

Die Bundesländer

Baden-Württemberg

- Fläche: 35.751,65 km^2
- Einwohner: 10.736.000
- Einwohner pro km^2: 300
- Hauptstadt (Einwohner): Stuttgart (593.923)
- Andere große Städte (Einwohner): Mannheim (307.914), Karlsruhe (286.327), Freiburg im Breisgau (217.547)

Das nach Bayern und Niedersachsen drittgrößte Bundesland liegt ganz im Südwesten. Die südliche Landesgrenze zur Schweiz bilden der Bodensee und der Oberrhein. Entlang der Westgrenze zu Frankreich erstreckt sich die Oberrheinische Tiefebene, eine Grabenbruchzone der Erdkruste, in der sich einige erloschene Vulkane befinden (Kaiserstuhl). Östlich des Rheins liegen der Schwarzwald und der südliche Odenwald, im Ostteil Baden-Württembergs die Schwäbische Alb. Kulturelle Sehenswürdigkeiten sind das Kloster Maulbronn zwischen Schwarz- und Odenwald, die Insel Reichenau im Bodensee (beide sind Weltkulturerbe) und Heidelberg, das wegen seiner malerischen Lage im Neckartal und der romantischen Altstadt als eine der schönsten Städte Deutschlands gilt.

Baden-Württemberg

- Area: 35,751.65 km^2
- Population: 10,736,000
- Population per km^2: 300
- Capital city (population): Stuttgart (593,923)
- Main cities (population): Mannheim (307,914), Karlsruhe (286,327), Freiburg im Breisgau (217,547)

The third-largest federal state after Bavaria and Lower Saxony lies in the southwest of Germany. Lake Constance and the Upper Rhine form its southern border with Switzerland. The Upper Rhine valley, a fracture zone on the earth's crust, stretches along the western border with France. A few extinct volcanoes are situated in the Kaiserstuhl area. The Black Forest and the southern Oden Forest lie to the east of the Rhine, and in the eastern part of Baden-Württemberg is the Swabian Alb area. Cultural landmarks include the Maulbronn Monastery between the Black Forest and Oden Forest, the island of Reichenau on Lake Constance (both are World Heritage Sites) and Heidelberg, which is considered one of the most beautiful towns in Germany due to its picturesque location in the Neckar valley and its romantic old town.

Bayern

- Fläche: 70.551,75 km^2
- Einwohner: 12.469.000
- Einwohner pro km^2: 177
- Hauptstadt (Einwohner): München (1.294.608)
- Andere große Städte (Einwohner): Nürnberg (500.855), Augsburg (262.512), Würzburg (134.913)

Das größte deutsche Bundesland wird im Süden von den Nördlichen Kalkalpen begrenzt, zu denen auch Deutschlands höchster Berg, die Zugspitze (2962 Meter), gehört. Alle Flüsse, die hier entspringen, fließen nach Norden zur Donau. Dazwischen liegt das von Eiszeitgletschern geformte Alpenvorland, eine hügelige Moränenlandschaft mit zahlreichen Seen (Chiemsee, Starnberger See, Ammersee u. a.). Nördlich der Donau folgt Mittelgebirgsland: der Bayerische Wald, der Oberpfälzer Wald und das Fichtelgebirge im Osten und das Schwäbisch-Fränkische Stufenland mit Steigerwald und Fränkischer Alb im Norden. Die Landeshauptstadt München ist die drittgrößte Stadt Deutschlands und berühmt für ihr Oktoberfest, ihre vielen Museen (Deutsches Museum, Pinakotheken) und architektonischen Sehenswürdigkeiten (Frauenkirche, Olympiastadion). Für Kulturfreunde lohnt sich auch ein Besuch Augsburgs und Nürnbergs oder der Altstädte von Regensburg und Bamberg, die beide zum Weltkulturerbe zählen.

Bavaria

- Area: 70,551.75 km^2
- Population: 12,469,000
- Population per km^2: 177
- Capital city (population): Munich (1,294,608)
- Main cities (population): Nuremberg (500,855), Augsburg (262,512), Würzburg (134,913)

The largest German federal state's southern border is formed by the Northern Limestone Alps, to which Germany's highest mountain – the Zugspitze (2962 metres) – belongs. Every river that rises here flows northwards towards the Danube. In between, the Alpenvorland is a hilly moraine landscape formed by the glaciers of the ice age, which has numerous lakes including the Chiemsee, Starnberg Lake and Ammersee. To the north of the Danube lie the low level mountain ranges of the Bavarian Forest, the Upper Palatinate Forest and the Fichtel Mountains in the east, and the Swabian-Franconian escarpment with the Steiger Forest and the Franconian Jura in the north. Bavaria's capital Munich is the third-largest city in Germany and is famous for the Oktoberfest, its many museums (Deutsches Museum, the Pinakothek art galleries) and architectural landmarks such as the Frauenkirche and the Olympic Stadium. For culture enthusiasts it is well worth a visit to Augsburg and Nuremberg or the old towns of Regensburg and Bamberg, both of which are World Heritage Sites.

Berlin

- Fläche: 891,85 km^2
- Einwohner: 3.395.000
- Einwohner pro km^2: 3807

Deutschlands größte Stadt ist zugleich Bundeshauptstadt und ein eigenständiges Bundesland inmitten des Bundeslandes Brandenburg. Das Stadtzentrum entstand an der schmalsten Stelle des

Berlin

- Area: 891.85 km^2
- Population: 3,395,000
- Population per km^2: 3807

Germany's largest city is both the national capital and a federal state in its own right, surrounded by the state of Brandenburg. The city centre emerged at the narrowest point of the Warsaw-Berlin

eiszeitlichen Warschau-Berliner Urstromtals, das von der Spree durchflossen wird. Diese mündet im Westen der Stadt in die Havel, deren zahlreiche Ausbuchtungen (Großer und Kleiner Wannsee u.a.) beliebte Ausflugsziele der Berliner sind. Ein zweites wichtiges Naherholungsgebiet im Südosten ist der Müggelsee. In den Randzonen Berlins befinden sich ausgedehnte Wald- und Parkgebiete, aber ebenso wichtige Wirtschaftsstandorte, die für einige Stadtteile namensgebend waren (z.B. Siemensstadt). Die Innenstadt wartet mit zahlreichen touristischen Highlights auf, wie dem Brandenburger Tor, dem Reichstag, der Museumsinsel (Weltkulturerbe!) und dem artenreichsten Zoo der Welt.

Brandenburg

- Fläche: 29.478,61 km^2
- Einwohner: 2.559.000
- Einwohner pro km^2: 87
- Hauptstadt (Einwohner): Potsdam (148.813)
- Andere große Städte (Einwohner): Cottbus (103.837)

Das größte der sogenannten neuen Bundesländer liegt im Bereich des Norddeutschen Tieflandes und grenzt im Osten an Polen. Den Norden durchzieht ein Ausläufer des Baltischen Landrückens, eine Moränenlandschaft mit vielen Seen. Reich an Gewässern ist auch die Uckermark im Nordosten, wo in der Schorfheide eines der schönsten Waldgebiete Deutschlands besucht werden kann. Im Süden erheben sich Altmoränen (Fläming, Lausitzer Grenzwall). Die Flüsse Spree, Havel, Rihn, Dahme, teilweise auch die Elbe fließen durch Urstromtäler, die das Schmelzwasser der Eiszeitgletscher ausschwemmte. Hier finden sich Feuchtgebiete mit großen Auwäldern (Spreewald, Oderbruch). Kulturelles Highlight ist die Landeshauptstadt Potsdam, deren Schlösser (z.B. Sanssouci) und Parks zum Weltkulturerbe gehören.

ice age glacial valley, through which the River Spree flows. This flows in the west of the city into the Havel river, whose many offshoots (including the Large and Small Wannsee lakes) are popular leisure destinations for Berliners. Another important leisure area in the south east is the Müggelsee. On the edges of Berlin there are extensive areas of forest and parkland as well important business locations, which have provided the names for some parts of the city (for example Siemensstadt). The city centre has numerous tourist highlights such as the Brandenburg Gate, the Reichstag, the Museum Island (a World Heritage Site) and the most species-rich zoo in the world.

Brandenburg

- Area: 29,478.61 km^2
- Population: 2,559,000
- Population per km^2: 87
- Capital city (population): Potsdam (148,813)
- Main cities (population): Cottbus (103,837)

The largest of the ›new‹ federal states lies in the North German lowlands and borders with Poland to the east. The north of the state features an offshoot of the Baltic Ridge, which is a moraine landscape with many lakes. The Uckermark to the northeast also has many watercourses and you can visit one of Germany's most beautiful woodland areas there in the Schorfheide. To the south, ancient moraine landscapes arise, including Fläming and the Lusatian Grenzwall area. The Rivers Spree, Havel, Rihn, Dahme and, in places, the Elbe flow through the glacial valleys, which swept away the melt water from the ice age glaciers. This area is home to wetlands with large lowland forests (including the Spree Forest and the Oderbruch). The state capital Potsdam is a cultural highlight: its palaces (including the Palace of Sanssouci) and parks are World Heritage Sites.

Freie Hansestadt Bremen

- Fläche: 404,28 km^2
- Einwohner: 663.000
- Einwohner pro km^2: 1641
- Hauptstadt (Einwohner): Bremen (547.934)
- Andere große Städte (Einwohner): Bremerhaven (116.045)

Das kleinste Land Deutschlands trägt den Namen »Freie Hansestadt Bremen«, ist aber weder Land noch Stadt, sondern zwei Städte: die Hauptstadt Bremen und das rund 60 Kilometer nördlich gelegene Bremerhaven. Zwischen den beiden Städten liegt niedersächsisches Gebiet. Verbunden sind sie durch den Fluss Weser. Bremerhaven entstand Anfang des 19. Jahrhunderts, als die Unterweser so versandet war, dass Hochseeschiffe nicht mehr bis Bremen fahren konnten. Die Stadt kaufte deshalb ein Stück Nordseeküste und gründete dort einen neuen »Bremer Haven«. An der Stelle des ursprünglichen Hafens befindet sich heute das Deutsche Schifffahrtsmuseum, eines der weltweit bedeutendsten Museen seiner Art. Adresse Nummer eins für Kulturreisende in Bremen ist das gotische Rathaus mit seiner Fassade im Stil der Weserrenaissance (Weltkulturerbe).

Free Hanseatic City of Bremen

- Area: 404.28 km^2
- Population: 663,000
- Population per km^2: 1641
- Capital city (population): Bremen (547,934)
- Main cities (population): Bremerhaven (116,045)

The smallest federal state in Germany is called the Free Hanseatic City of Bremen. In fact it is neither a state nor a city, but two cities – the capital Bremen and Bremerhaven which lies around 60 kilometres to the north. The area between the two belongs to Lower Saxony. The two are connected by the River Weser. Bremerhaven emerged at the beginning of the 19th century when the lower Weser was so silted up that ocean-going ships were no longer able to reach Bremen. Therefore the city bought a stretch of North Sea coastline and established a new 'Bremer Haven' or Port of Bremen there. Today on the site of the original port is the German Maritime Museum, one of the foremost museums of its kind in the world. The first port of call for culture buffs visiting Bremen is the Gothic town hall with its façade in the style of the Weser Renaissance (a World Heritage Site).

Freie und Hansestadt Hamburg

- Fläche: 755,16 km^2
- Einwohner: 1.744.000
- Einwohner pro km^2: 2309

Die Freie und Hansestadt Hamburg, Deutschlands zweitgrößte Stadt nach Berlin, liegt an der Mündung der Alster und der Bille in die Elbe. Die Alster ist im Zentrum zum Alstersee aufgestaut, der sich in Binnen- und Außenalster teilt. Obwohl 110 Kilometer von der Elbmündung in die Nordsee entfernt, machen sich die Gezeiten

Free and Hanseatic City of Hamburg

- Area: 755.16 km^2
- Population: 1,744,000
- Population per km^2: 2309

The Free and Hanseatic City of Hamburg is Germany's second-largest city after Berlin. It lies at the confluence of the Rivers Alster and Bille into the River Elbe. The Alster is dammed in the city centre to form the Alstersee, which is divided into the Binnenalster (inner Alster) and Außenalster (outer Alster). Although it is 110 kilometres

noch in Hamburg bemerkbar. Der Hamburger Hafen, ein offener Tidehafen, ist nach jenem von Rotterdam der zweitgrößte Seehafen Europas. Unzählige Bäche und Kanäle bestimmen neben den großen Flüssen das Stadtbild: Mit 2500 Brücken ist Hamburg die brückenreichste Stadt Europas. Kulturhistorisch interessant sind die auf Eichenpfählen erbaute Speicherstadt mit ihren hundert Jahre alten denkmalgeschützten Lagerhäusern und das Wahrzeichen der Stadt, die barocke St.-Michaelis-Kirche, kurz »Michel« genannt.

Hessen

- Fläche: 21.114,79 km^2
- Einwohner: 6.092.000
- Einwohner pro km^2: 289
- Hauptstadt (Einwohner): Wiesbaden (275.562)
- Andere große Städte (Einwohner): Frankfurt am Main (652.610), Kassel (193.518), Darmstadt (141.257)

Der größte Teil Hessens liegt im Bereich der deutschen Mittelgebirge: Taunus, Hoher Westerwald, Gladenbacher Bergland im Westen, Hessisches Bergland im Osten und Spessart und Odenwald im Süden. Der Vogelsberg im Zentrum, ein erloschener Vulkan, ist das größte zusammenhängende Basaltmassiv Europas. Hessen ist eines der fließgewässerreichsten Bundesländer. Die wichtigsten Flüsse sind Main, Lahn, Neckar, Fulda, Eder, Weser und Werra, die Westgrenze bildet der Rhein. Größte Stadt und wirtschaftliches Zentrum ist Frankfurt am Main. Hessen wartet mit mehreren UNESCO-Weltkultur- und -naturerben auf: der einzigartigen Fossilienfundstätte Grube Messel, dem Obergermanisch-Raetischen Limes (der Nordgrenze des Römischen Reichs) und dem Kloster Lorsch mit seiner aus karolingischer Zeit stammenden Torhalle.

away from the Elbe estuary on the North Sea coast, the tides are still evident in Hamburg. Hamburg's port, an open tidal harbour, is the second-largest sea port in Europe after Rotterdam. As well as the major rivers, countless streams and canals define the cityscape – with its 2500 bridges, Hamburg has more bridges than any other town in Europe. From a cultural heritage point of view, the Speicherstadt is interesting, with its hundred-year-old protected warehouses constructed on oak piles, as well as the emblem of the city, the baroque St Michaelis Church, known simply as 'Michel'.

Hesse

- Area: 21,114.79 km^2
- Population: 6,092,000
- Population per km^2: 289
- Capital city (population): Wiesbaden (275,562)
- Main cities (population): Frankfurt am Main (652,610), Kassel (193,518), Darmstadt (141,257)

Most of Hesse lies in and around the German low mountain ranges. These include the Taunus, High Westerwald and Gladenbach Highlands to the west; the Hessian Highlands in the east and the Spessart and Oden Forest to the south. The Vogelsberg, an extinct volcano, is located in the centre of the state. It is the largest continuous basalt massif in Europe. Hesse is one of the most river-rich federal states. The key rivers are the Main, Lahn, Neckar, Fulda, Eder, Weser and Werra, while the Rhine forms its western border. Frankfurt am Main is the biggest city and economic centre. Hesse has several UNESCO World Heritage Sites, including the unique Messel Pit Fossil Site, the Upper German-Raetian Limes (the northern border of the Roman Empire) and the Lorsch Monastery with its 'Torhalle' or gatehouse dating back to the Carolingian era.

Mecklenburg-Vorpommern

- Fläche: 23.180,14 km^2
- Einwohner: 1.707.000
- Einwohner pro km^2: 74
- Hauptstadt (Einwohner): Schwerin (96.280)
- Andere große Städte (Einwohner): Rostock (199.868)

Das heutige Bundesland entstand nach dem Zweiten Weltkrieg durch Zusammenschluss der Regionen Mecklenburg und Vorpommern. Seine Landeshauptstadt Schwerin ist mit nur 100 000 Einwohnern die kleinste Hauptstadt eines deutschen Bundeslandes. 1700 km Ostseeküste begrenzen das Land im Norden. Die Landschaft ist überwiegend flach. Höchste Erhebung sind die Helpter Berge (179 m). Den zentralen und südlichen Teil des Landes nimmt die von Eiszeitgletschern geformte Mecklenburgische Seenplatte ein. Sie besteht aus rund tausend Seen, deren größte die Müritz, der Schweriner See und der Plauer See sind. Die Seenplatte, die Ostseeküste mit den vorgelagerten Inseln (Rügen) und zahlreiche Naturschutzgebiete (darunter die drei Nationalparks Müritz, Vorpommersche Boddenlandschaft und Jasmund) machen Mecklenburg-Vorpommern zu einem der schönsten Urlaubsgebiete Deutschlands. Zum Weltkulturerbe zählen die mittelalterlichen Altstädte der ehemaligen Ostsee-Hansestädte Stralsund und Wismar.

Mecklenburg-Western Pomerania

- Area: 23,180.14 km^2
- Population: 1,707,000
- Population per km^2: 74
- Capital city (population): Schwerin (96,280)
- Main cities (population): Rostock (199,868)

The federal state as it is today emerged after the Second World War from the amalgamation of the regions of Mecklenburg and West Pomerania. Its capital Schwerin is the smallest capital city of any German federal state with only 100,000 residents. The state is bordered to the north by 1700 km of Baltic Sea coast. The landscape is predominantly flat and the Helpter Hills form the highest point at 179 m. The central and southern regions of the state take in the Mecklenburg lake district, which was formed by ice age glaciers. It has around one thousand lakes, of which the Müritz, Schwerin Lake and Plauer Lake are the largest. The lake district, the Baltic coast with its islands (Rügen) and numerous nature conservation areas (including the three National Parks of Müritz, West-Pomeranian Boddenlandschaft and Jasmund) make Mecklenburg-Western Pomerania one of the most beautiful holiday areas in Germany. The medieval old town centres of the former Baltic Hanseatic towns of Stralsund and Wismar are World Heritage Sites.

Niedersachsen

- Fläche: 47.624,20 km^2
- Einwohner: 7.994.000
- Einwohner pro km^2: 168
- Hauptstadt (Einwohner): Hannover (516.343)
- Andere große Städte (Einwohner): Braunschweig (245.467), Osnabrück (163.020), Oldenburg (159.060)

Das zweitgrößte Bundesland, das im Westen an die Niederlande grenzt, gehört zum Norddeutschen Tiefland. Es reicht von den Mittelgebirgen im Süden (Harz, Weserbergland, Leinebergland) bis zur Nordseeküste und den Ostfriesischen Inseln (Borkum, Norderney, Langeoog u. a.), die im Nationalpark Niedersächsisches Wattenmeer liegen. Die wichtigsten Flüsse sind die Ems, die Weser und die Elbe, die eine natürliche Landesgrenze im Nordosten darstellt. Eine einmalige alte Kulturlandschaft ist die Lüneburger Heide mit Heideflächen und Hochmooren. Kulturhistorisch bedeutende Ziele (UNESCO-Welterbe) sind Hildesheim mit der romanischen Michaeliskirche, die Altstadt von Goslar und das nahe Goslar gelegene Erzbergwerk Rammelsberg, das heute ein Museum ist.

Nordrhein-Westfalen

- Fläche: 34.085,29 km^2
- Einwohner: 18.058.000
- Einwohner pro km^2: 530
- Hauptstadt (Einwohner): Düsseldorf (577.505)
- Andere große Städte (Einwohner): Köln (989.766), Dortmund (587.624), Essen (583.198), Duisburg (499.111)

Das nur viertgrößte, aber bevölkerungsreichste deutsche Bundesland grenzt im Westen an Belgien und die Niederlande. Der Norden ist geprägt vom Norddeutschen Tiefland. Der größte Teil des Landes

Lower Saxony

- Area: 47,624.20 km^2
- Population: 7,994,000
- Population per km^2: 168
- Capital city (population): Hanover (516,343)
- Main cities (population): Braunschweig (245,467), Osnabrück (163,020), Oldenburg (159,060)

The second-largest federal state, which borders with the Netherlands to the west, is part of the North German lowlands. It stretches from the low level mountains in the south (including the Harz, Weser Highlands and Leine Highlands) to the North Sea coast and the East Friesian Islands (including Borkum, Norderney, Langeoog), which are situated in the Wadden Sea National Park of Lower Saxony. The main rivers are the Ems, Weser and the Elbe, the latter of which creates a natural state boundary in the north east. Lüneburg Heath offers a unique, traditional cultural landscape with its heathland and upland moors. Of cultural significance for their UNESCO World Heritage Sites are Hildesheim with its Romanesque Michaelis Church, the old town centre of Goslar and the neighbouring Rammelsberg ore mine, which is a museum today.

North Rhine-Westphalia

- Area: 34,085.29 km^2
- Population: 18,058,000
- Population per km^2: 530
- Capital city (population): Düsseldorf (577,505)
- Main cities (population): Cologne (989,766), Dortmund (587,624), Essen (583,198), Duisburg (499,111)

It is only the fourth-largest in area but is the most densely populated German federal state and it borders to the west with Belgium and the Netherlands. The north is characterised by the

liegt im Bereich des Stromgebiets des Rheins. Im Zentrum liegt das Ruhrgebiet, der größte Ballungsraum Deutschlands, in dem Städte wie Duisburg, Essen, Gelsenkirchen, Bochum und Dortmund fließend ineinander übergehen. Im Süden hat Nordrhein-Westfalen Anteil am Rheinischen Schiefergebirge (Eifel, Sauerland, Bergisches Land, Siegerland, Siebengebirge), im Norden am Weserbergland. Kulturhistorisch bedeutend sind Aachen, die Stadt Karls des Großen, und Köln. Neben den Domen dieser beiden Städte wurden auch die Schlösser Augustusburg und Falkenlust in Brühl und die Industrieanlage Zeche Zollverein in Essen in den Rang eines Weltkulturerbes erhoben.

North German lowlands. The largest part of the state lies in the area of the Rhine basin. The Ruhr area is in the centre of the state and is the biggest conurbation in Germany. Its cities, including Duisburg, Essen, Gelsenkirchen, Bochum and Dortmund, all merge into one another. To the south of North Rhine-Westphalia lies part of the Rhenish Uplands (including the hills of the Eifel, Sauerland, Bergisches Land, Siegerland and the Siebengebirge); to the north lies part of the Weser Highlands. Aachen, the city of Charlemagne, is of cultural significance, as is Cologne. As well as the cathedrals of both these cities, the palaces of Augustusburg and Falkenlust in Brühl and the Zollverein Coal Mine Industrial Complex in Essen are listed as World Heritage Sites.

Rheinland-Pfalz

- Fläche: 19.853,36 km^2
- Einwohner: 4.059.000
- Einwohner pro km^2: 204
- Hauptstadt (Einwohner): Mainz (196.425)
- Andere große Städte (Einwohner): Ludwigshafen am Rhein (163.560), Koblenz (105.888)

Rhineland-Palatinate

- Area: 19,853.36 km^2
- Population: 4,059,000
- Population per km^2: 204
- Capital city (population): Mainz (196,425)
- Main cities (population): Ludwigshafen am Rhein (163,560), Koblenz (105,888)

Das Bundesland, das im Westen an Luxemburg und Belgien grenzt, liegt großteils im Bereich der Mittelgebirge. Im Norden befindet sich das Rheinische Schiefergebirge (Eifel, Hunsrück, Westerwald, Hintertaunus), im Süden der Pfälzer Wald. Größte Flüsse sind die Mosel und der Rhein, der nordwärts durch die Oberrheinische Tiefebene strömt. Naturfreunde können auf der Deutschen Vulkanstraße die Eifel erkunden, eine von Vulkankegeln, Maaren und Calderen (Laacher See) geprägte Landschaft. Kulturfreunde dürfen Trier nicht verpassen, das wie die Landeshauptstadt Mainz auf eine römische Siedlung zurückgeht. Die römischen Bauten, die in Trier erhalten sind (Amphitheater,

Bordering on Luxembourg and Belgium in the west, this federal state lies largely in the area of the low level mountains. The Rhenish Uplands (with the Eifel, Hunsrück, Westerwald and Hintertaunus) lie to the north, while the Palatinate Forest lies to the south. The largest rivers are the Moselle and the Rhine, which flows northwards through the Upper Rhine valley. On the German Volcano Route, nature enthusiasts can explore the Eifel, a landscape characterised by lava domes, maars and calderas (such as the Laach Lake). Culture buffs should not miss Trier which, like the state capital Mainz, dates back to a roman settlement. The roman remains in Trier (the amphitheatre, thermal baths

Thermen, Porta Nigra), sind ebenso Weltkulturerbe wie der Dom von Speyer, das größte und bedeutendste romanische Bauwerk Deutschlands.

Saarland

- Fläche: 2.568,70 km²
- Einwohner: 1.050.000
- Einwohner pro km²: 409
- Hauptstadt (Einwohner): Saarbrücken (177.870)

Das, abgesehen von den Stadtstaaten Berlin, Bremen und Hamburg, kleinste deutsche Bundesland liegt im Südwesten und grenzt an Frankreich und Luxemburg. Der längste Fluss ist die Saar, nach der das Land und die Landeshauptstadt Saarbrücken benannt sind. Den größten Teil nimmt das im Zentrum gelegene hügelige Saar-Nahe-Bergland ein. Im Norden hat das Saarland Anteil am Hunsrück (Schwarzwälder Hochwald). Ein Drittel seiner Fläche ist von Laub- und Mischwäldern bedeckt, was das Saarland zu einem der waldreichsten Bundesländer macht. Aufgrund großer Steinkohlevorkommen bestimmten der Bergbau und die Stahlverarbeitung lange das wirtschaftliche Leben. Einen Eindruck davon bekommt man im ehemaligen Eisenwerk Völklinger Hütte, das die UNESCO 1994 als weltweit erstes Industriedenkmal zum Weltkulturerbe ernannte.

and the Porta Nigra) are World Heritage Sites, as is Speyer Cathedral, the largest and most significant Romanesque construction in Germany.

Saarland

- Area: 2,568.70 km²
- Population: 1,050,000
- Population per km²: 409
- Capital city (population): Saarbrücken (177,870)

Apart from the city states of Berlin, Bremen and Hamburg, this is Germany's smallest federal state. It lies in the south west of Germany and borders with France and Luxembourg. The Saar is its longest river and both the state and capital city of Saarbrücken take their names from it. The Saar-Nahe hills in the middle of the state take up a large part of its area. Part of the Hunsrück (Black Forest Hochwald) lies in the north of Saarland. One third of its area is covered with deciduous and mixed forest, making Saarland one of the most wooded federal states. Due to large coal deposits, mining and steelworks were for a long time the key industries here. You get a feel for this by visiting the former ironworks of Völklingen, which in 1994 became the first industrial UNESCO World Heritage Site.

Sachsen

- Fläche: 18.415,51 km²
- Einwohner: 4.274.000
- Einwohner pro km²: 232
- Hauptstadt (Einwohner): Dresden (504.795)
- Andere große Städte (Einwohner): Leipzig (506.578), Chemnitz (245.700)

Das östlichste deutsche Bundesland grenzt im Osten an Polen und im Süden an Tschechien. Im Süden hat Sachsen Anteil an den deutschen Mittelgebirgen: am Elstergebirge, am Erzgebirge, am Elbsandsteingebirge, in dem der Nationalpark Sächsische Schweiz liegt, und am Lausitzer Gebirge, dessen sächsischer Teil Zittauer Gebirge heißt. Nach Norden hin folgen Hügelland, das von eiszeitlichen Moränen geprägt ist, und dann Flachland (die Leipziger Tieflandbucht und der nördliche Teil der Oberlausitz). Der größte Fluss ist die Elbe, die Sachsen von Südosten nach Nordwesten durchfließt. Das Dresdner Elbtal wurde wegen seiner einmaligen Verbindung aus Naturlandschaft und Kulturstätte (Dresdner Altstadt) von der UNESCO zum Welterbe erklärt.

Saxony

- Area: 18,415.51 km²
- Population: 4,274,000
- Population per km²: 232
- Capital city (population): Dresden (504,795)
- Main cities (population): Leipzig (506,578), Chemnitz (245,700)

The easternmost German federal state borders with Poland in the east and the Czech Republic in the south. The south of Saxony is home to parts of the German low level mountains, including the Elstergebirge, the Ore Mountains, the Elbe Sandstone Mountains (home of the Saxon Switzerland National Park), and the Lusatian Mountains, of which the Saxon section is called the Zittau Mountains. To the north lies hilly countryside, characterised by ice age moraines, then the plains of the Leipzig lowland basin and the northern part of Upper Lusatia. The largest river is the Elbe, which flows through Saxony from the southeast to the northwest. The Dresden Elbe Valley was declared a World Heritage Site by UNESCO due to its unique combination of natural landscape and the cultural interest of Dresden's old town.

Sachsen-Anhalt

- Fläche: 20.446,31 km²
- Einwohner: 2.470.000
- Einwohner pro km²: 121
- Hauptstadt (Einwohner): Magdeburg (229.826)
- Andere große Städte (Einwohner): Chemnitz (245.700), Halle an der Saale (235.720)

Sachsen-Anhalt erstreckt sich beiderseits der Mittelelbe, die das Land nach Norden hin durchfließt. Im Norden liegt die Altmark, die zum Norddeutschen Tiefland gehört. Das Zentrum bildet

Saxony-Anhalt

- Area: 20,446.31 km²
- Population: 2,470,000
- Population per km²: 121
- Capital city (population): Magdeburg (229,826)
- Main cities (population): Chemnitz (245,700), Halle an der Saale (235,720)

Saxony-Anhalt takes in both sides of the Middle Elbe, which flows through the state to the north. The Altmark area, part of the North German lowlands, lies to the north. The centre is formed by the

die Magdeburger Börde, eine fruchtbare Lösslandschaft. Im Süden hat Sachsen-Anhalt Anteil am Harz und an der Leipziger Tieflandbucht. Größte Stadt und wirtschaftliches Zentrum ist Halle im Südosten. Gleich fünf Orte zählen zum UNESCO-Welterbe: die Martin-Luther-Städte Wittenberg und Eisleben, das mittelalterliche Quedlinburg, Dessau mit wichtigen Bauten der Bauhaus-Schule und das Dessau-Wörlitzer Gartenreich, eine einmalige Parklandschaft mit Schlössern im Biosphärenreservat Mittelelbe.

Schleswig-Holstein

- Fläche: 15.799,38 km²
- Einwohner: 2.833
- Einwohner pro km²: 179
- Hauptstadt (Einwohner): Kiel (235.366)
- Andere große Städte (Einwohner): Lübeck (211.213)

Das nördlichste deutsche Bundesland, das von der Nordsee bis zur Ostsee reicht, wird auch »Land zwischen den Meeren« genannt. Im Norden grenzt es an Dänemark. Landschaftlich gliedert sich Schleswig-Holstein in flaches Schwemmland (Marsch) im Westen, sandige Geest in der Mitte und das von eiszeitlichen Moränen geprägte Hügelland im Osten. Vor der stark zergliederten Ostseeküste liegt die Insel Fehmarn. Entlang der Nordseeküste erstreckt sich das Wattenmeer mit den Nordfriesischen Inseln (Sylt, Föhr, Amrum u. a.). Auch Helgoland, das gut 40 Kilometer vom Festland entfernt liegt, gehört zu Schleswig-Holstein. Für Kulturfreunde eine Reise wert sind die Ausgrabungsstätte Haithabu nebst Wikingermuseum ganz im Norden und die Altstadt von Lübeck, die zum Weltkulturerbe zählt.

Magdeburg Börde, a fertile loess plain. In the south of Saxony-Anhalt are the Harz Mountains and the Leipzig lowland basin. Halle is the largest city and economic centre in the south-east of the state. The state is home to five UNESCO World Heritage Sites, including the Luther Memorials in Wittenberg and Eisleben, the medieval town of Quedlinburg, Dessau with its important Bauhaus School buildings and the Garden Kingdom of Dessau-Wörlitz, a unique parkland area with palaces in the Middle Elbe Biosphere Reserve.

Schleswig-Holstein

- Area: 15,799.38 km²
- Population: 2,833
- Population per km²: 179
- Capital city (population): Kiel (235,366)
- Main cities (population): Lübeck (211,213)

The most northerly German federal state, which stretches from the North Sea to the Baltic Sea, is also known as the 'Land between the seas'. To the north it borders with Denmark. The landscape of Schleswig-Holstein divides into flat alluvial landscapes, or marshland, in the west, sandy geest soil in the centre and to the east, hilly moraine landscapes dating back to the ice age. The island of Fehmarn lies off the ragged Baltic coast. The Wadden Sea, with the North Friesian Islands that include Sylt, Föhr and Amrum, stretches along the North Sea coast. Heligoland, which lies some 40 kilometres off the mainland, also belongs to Schleswig-Holstein. For culture lovers, it is worth a taking a trip to the archaeological excavation site of Haithabu, together with its Viking museum in the north of the state, as well as the old town of Lübeck, which is a World Heritage Site.

Thüringen

- Fläche: 16.172,10 km^2
- Einwohner: 2.335.000
- Einwohner pro km^2: 144
- Hauptstadt (Einwohner): Erfurt (202.658)
- Andere große Städte (Einwohner): Gera (102.733), Jena (102.494)

Geografisch liegt Thüringen genau in der Mitte Deutschlands. Es ist umgeben von Bayern, Hessen, Niedersachsen, Sachsen und Sachsen-Anhalt. Im Norden hat Thüringen Anteil am Harz, im Süden liegen der Thüringer Wald und das Thüringer Schiefergebirge. Die größten Flüsse sind die Werra im Osten und die Saale im Westen. Interessante Ziele für Naturfreunde sind der Nationalpark Hainich, in dem ein von Buchen geprägter Urwald wächst, und das Biosphärenreservat Vessertal im Thüringerwald mit seiner einzigartigen Gebirgsflora. Kulturell bedeutend (Welterbe) sind Goethes Weimar und die Wartburg bei Eisenach.

Thuringia

- Area: 16,172.10 km^2
- Population: 2,335,000
- Population per km^2: 144
- Capital city (population): Erfurt (202,658)
- Main cities (population): Gera (102,733), Jena (102,494)

Geographically speaking, Thuringia lies right in the middle of Germany. It is surrounded by Bavaria, Hesse, Lower Saxony, Saxony and Saxony-Anhalt. In the north of Thuringia lies part of the Harz Mountains, while to the south are the Thuringian Forest and the Thuringian Slate Mountains. The main rivers are the Werra in the east and the Saale in the west. Nature enthusiasts will be interested in the Hainich National Park, with its ancient forest dominated by beech trees, as well as the Vessertal Biosphere Reserve in the Thuringian Forest with its unique mountain flora. Of cultural importance (World Heritage Sites) are Goethe's Weimar and Wartburg Castle near Eisenach.

Quelle: © Statistische Ämter des Bundes und der Länder

Bibliografische Information Der Deutschen Nationalbibliothek
Die Deutsche Nationalbibliothek verzeichnet diese Publikation in der Deutschen Nationalbibliografie; detaillierte bibliografische Daten sind im Internet unter http://dnb.d-nb.de abrufbar.

Deutsche Erstausgabe

Die Bildauswahl dieser Ausgabe basiert auf dem erstmals 2004 im Knesebeck Verlag erschienenen Band *Deutschland von oben – Tag für Tag* von Gerhard Launer. Die Texte zu den Bildern und die Darstellung der Bundesländer im Anhang wurden von Gernot Geurtzen verfasst.

Übersetzung der Texte ins Englische: Lesley Forner

Gestaltung: Typoly, Berlin
Umschlaggestaltung: Fabian Arnet
Satz: satz & repro Grieb, München
Druck: Uhl, Radolfzell
Printed in Germany

ISBN 978-3-89660-554-2

www.knesebeck-verlag.de